Cerf, Bennett

Bennett Cerf's treasury of
atrocious puns

DATE DUE

JL 8 '85			
AUG. 25			
JUL 13 '88			
JUN 13 '9			
JUL 3 0 '92			
JA 30 '96			
OCT 0 8 '96			

Bennett Cerf's

TREASURY

OF

ATROCIOUS

PUNS

BY BENNETT CERF

LAUGH DAY

RIDDLE-DE-DEE

OUT ON A LIMERICK

THE LAUGH'S ON ME

READING FOR PLEASURE

THE LIFE OF THE PARTY

AN ENCYCLOPEDIA OF MODERN AMERICAN HUMOR

GOOD FOR A LAUGH

LAUGHTER INCORPORATED

SHAKE WELL BEFORE USING

LAUGHING STOCK

TRY AND STOP ME

Bennett Cerf's
TREASURY
OF
ATROCIOUS
PUNS

With Illustrations by Michael K. Frith

1817

Harper & Row, Publishers

New York, Evanston, and London

FIRST EDITION

LIBRARY OF CONGRESS CATALOG CARD NUMBER: 68-29571

K-S

CONTENTS

A *Foreword by the Publishers* 7

1. A THUMBNAIL HISTORY OF PUNMANSHIP 11

2. WHO'S ZOO 17
    PUNS ABOUT ANIMALS

3. WORDS ON PLAYS 25
    PUNS ABOUT SHOW BUSINESS

4. . . . AND PLAYS ON WORDS 32
    PUNS ABOUT SEMANTICS

5. SIGN LANGUAGE 37
    PUNS IN SIGNS

6. DAFFYNITIONS 39
    BY WEBSTER? NOAH, NOAH!

7. OPUNING OF THE GATES 42
    PUNS ABOUT CHILDREN AND THEIR EDUCATION

8. LOVE AND MARRIAGE 50
    PUNS ABOUT SEX

9. HOT CROSS PUNS 56
    PUNS ABOUT FOOD AND DRINK

10. PUNNY BUSINESS 62
    PUNS ABOUT COMMERCE AND HIGH LIFE

11. DRY DOCS 67
    PUNS ABOUT MEDICOS AND HOSPITALS

12. CRIME AND PUN-ISHMENT   70
    PUNS ABOUT THE LAW

13. SOME FOR THE BOOK   74
    PUNS ABOUT THE LITERARY WORLD

14. NARY A FALSE NOTE   82
    PUNS ABOUT MUSIC AND MUSICIANS

15. FAIR GAME   85
    PUNS ABOUT SPORTS

16. PUNDEMONIUM   89
    VERY SHORT PUNS FOR PEOPLE IN A HURRY

17. WHEN PUNSTERS GET VERSE   96
    PUNS IN RHYME

18. RIDDLE-DE-DEES   98
    PUNS IN RIDDLE FORM

19. AROUND THE WORLD IN EIGHTY PUNS   101

A FOREWORD BY THE PUBLISHERS

BENNETT CERF, sometime distinguished publisher, author, lecturer, and television "personality," is also the country's champion and unquenchable perpetrator of puns. To countless Americans who suffer from the same affliction he is a friend indeed. They can evade a small measure of culpability for every horrendous pun THEY spawn by winding it up with a resigned "Even Bennett Cerf wouldn't stoop as low as THAT!" They're wrong.

Here, in one awe-inspiring volume, are all the puns Mr. Cerf has hoarded over the years. Some were written for the *Saturday Review*, *This Week*, King Features, *Reader's Digest*, and *Playboy*. Some crept into his previous best-selling compendiums of humor. Some were inflicted on his long-suffering "What's My Line" confrere, John Charles Daly. Many never have appeared in print before. Dozens never should have appeared in print at all. But there al-

7

ways will be somebody to chuckle wholeheartedly at the very worst of them—as long as Mr. Cerf is around, at any rate.

One last warning: Don't—PLEASE—don't read too many of these puns at one sitting. There's a limit to EVERY human's endurance.

(Signed) Mr. HARPER
Mr. Row

Reluctantly O.K.'d
by Mr. Cerf
Mount Kisco, New York
August, 1968

Bennett Cerf's

TREASURY

OF

ATROCIOUS

PUNS

A THUMBNAIL HISTORY OF PUNMANSHIP

THE OUTRAGEOUS and obviously baseless charge that a pun is the lowest form of wit finally has been traced back to its source: a mean, shriveled Egyptian curmudgeon about 3000 B.C. who had no sense of humor whatever and furthermore was hard of hearing. He just sat on a bank of the Nile glowering, licking his Cheops, and groaning every time his neighbor, a splendid chap named Rameses Cerf IV, let a pun drop.

...when who should barge in but Cleopatra! "I want my Mummy!" she shouted...

The inveterate punster learns early not to be disconcerted when his best efforts are met, at best, by grim silence and, at worst, by outright abuse. Anybody who considers himself a sophisticate (and who doesn't?) knows it is not fashionable to laugh at a pun. He also knows, however, that the listener who registers the most vehement contempt is the one who'll be on the phone fastest to broadcast the pun as his own creation.

The first pun ever made is credited, logically enough, to Adam. Eve teased him, "What's wrong with eating this little old apple?" and Adam answered, "I'll bite." The next day they both were bounced out of the Garden of Eden.

When Athens was at the pinnacle of its glory, the poet Homer was heard yodeling, "I love, I love, I love my wife—but oh, Euclid!" And in Rome, the great Caesar (roamin'est noble of them all), when asked by his friend Brutus at the Forum one afternoon, "How many hamburgers did you consume at luncheon today, Julius?" couldn't resist answering, "Et two, Brute."

It was in Rome, too, that a pun-dit only recently discovered what Cleopatra really whispered to Mark Antony when he asked her if she was true to him (silly boy!). Cleo swore, "Omar Khayyám!"

You have read a lot about the knights of King Arthur who fared forth on coal-black chargers to rescue beautiful maidens from dragons' clutches, but did you ever know that one of them was mounted on a St. Bernard dog? His name was Sir Marmaduke, and he and the St. Bernard performed many a deed of derring-do. One evening, however, they were caught in a torrential thunderstorm, and sought shelter at a nearby tavern. "Reservation?" asked the room clerk. "No," admitted Sir Marmaduke. "Sorry," said the clerk, "no room without a reservation." It was at this moment that he discovered that Marmaduke was sitting astride his faithful St. Bernard. "Hold on," said the clerk. "We'll have to find *something* for you. I wouldn't put out a knight on a dog like this."

In ancient Burma, legend has it that a hunter was tracking game so avidly one day in the steaming jungle that his false teeth fell out. Ever since, the unfortunate wretch has been searching for his bridge on the River Kwai.

Shakespeare's plays, of course, are larded with puns, though it's an intrepid soul today who will claim he understands one in ten of them. They refer to personages and customs long since forgotten, so the punch lines, no matter how boisterously delivered, are meaningless. By the same token, a pun that is priceless in 1969 may be utterly worthless a year later. How long, for instance, are people likely to chuckle over the rumor that France is taking over the Rock of Gibraltar—and renaming it de Gaulle Stone?

Speaking of Shakespeare, the immortal playwright decided one unreasonably hot day in the spring of 1595 to suspend writing sonnets to the girl next door and take her for a swim at a nearby British beach resort. They had to don swimsuits from their previous season's regalia, of course, and it suddenly occurred to Shakespeare that moths very possibly had been feeding on the back of his trunks. "Wouldst investigate, my love?" he asked his companion. She made a thorough, if unobtrusive search, then reported cheerfully, "No holes, Bard."

It was at the court of Versailles in France that King Louis XV noticed one evening that one of Madame Pompadour's fourteen petticoats was sagging. "Pompy," he informed her gallantly, "your quelque shows." And when, later, the royal barge capsized in the Seine, and the royal mistress asked if her precious kittens had been rescued, Louis had to tell her, "Hélas! Un, deux, trois, cats sank."

When Warren G. Harding was President of the U.S.A., he is alleged to have swallowed one evening by mistake four pages of the *Congressional Record*. He rushed to the medicine chest for relief. "What on earth are you up to?" called Mrs. Harding. Her husband explained tersely, "Boring from within." President Truman rarely overlooked a chance to take a few cronies home to Independence for a spot of his wife Bess's superb cooking. As he put it, "Missouri loves company."

When President Eisenhower replaced Truman, bridge became the favorite pastime at the White House. In one session, a daring Eisenhower finesse failed and he went down four tricks—doubled and vulnerable. "This," reflected the hale chief, "is one of the few times anybody around here has set a president."

In the McCarthy era, when everybody in public life had to be careful watching his appease and accuse, two young men named Roy Cohn and David Schine kicked up a mighty ruckus in the State Department. A Washington savant suggested that a horse named Harvest Moon be presented to Mr. Schine. "I can see him now seated astride his new steed," said the savant dreamily. "The caption under the photograph in the newspapers, of course, will be 'Schine on Harvest Moon.' "

It was in Washington, too, that pundit Clifton Fadiman, steering a party of friends to a little Italian restaurant he had praised to the skies, discovered that he had misplaced the proprietor's card. "We'll have to eat elsewhere," mourned Fadiman. "I seem to have lost my Spaghettysburg Address."

You can hear many a pun sponsored when it's fair weather and good advertising fellows get together. It took an operative from auto-leasing agency No. 2, for instance, to discover just what a winsome Italian lass had to say when some dastard ravished her in the back seat of a rented sedan: "It's a Hertz!"

Aficionados of the pun divide their favorites roughly into two categories: the "quickies"—just a sentence or two—and the involved long-drawn-out sagas where the premise is usually even more ridiculous than the punch line. The mere buildup of one of these complicated fragments of calculated nonsense is enough to make an unimaginative listener end up with the heebie-jeebies. One Harvard graduate I know, in fact, sought help from the police. The man he wanted was a Phi Beta Copper.

There is a great deal to be said for both abbreviated puns and the more intricate ones—and heaven knows all of it is said in the pages following. Unless the prospect pleases you, cast this book forth right now and save yourself a lot of unnecessary pun-ishment!

My sincere concern brings to mind a day when one of

Random House's most elegant authoresses swept out into Madison Avenue and was almost upended by a bemused pedestrian. He apologized profusely, but she froze him with a look and muttered, "How gauche!" "Simply fine, lady," answered the pedestrian, then added solicitously, "How gauche it with you?"

2

WHO'S ZOO
Puns About Animals

"WHERE," SCOFFED a crotchety rhinoceros, "do you fool monkeys pick up all those wild rumors you keep circulating?" "We get them," explained one dignified monk, "over the apevine."

A youngster found a salamander in his back yard and put it into a tank with his pet alligator. The alligator promptly swallowed the salamander. "Something awful's happened," wailed the youngster to his mother. "Sally's in our alli!"

In an obviously enchanted forest near the home of Mrs. Mary O'Brian, in San Bernardino, lived two families of amiable, hard-working gnus, who often enjoyed picnicking together. Each family boasted one young mischief-maker, however, though each mother was convinced her own little gnu was the innocent dupe of his evil friend.

"You should punish that rascally brat of yours," shrilled

one mother finally. "A sound spanking might do him some good."

"Spank *my* son, indeed," huffed the other. "Why don't you go paddle your own gnu?"

Edmund Fuller Kent, Connecticut's gift to the world of letters, avers that one evening he brought home as food for his dog an Italian dish compounded of flour, cheese, and tomatoes. The thoughtful master tilted it against a door to make it more accessible for the lazy pooch. Then he summoned his wife and told her cheerfully, "There's no longer any need for you to plan that sightseeing trip to Italy next summer. Here, before your very eyes, is the leaning Pizza of Towser." Wow, sir!

Riding in a dogcart, one wire-haired terrier said to the other, "Heard from your beau lately?" "Yes, indeed," was the reply. "I had a litter from him Tuesday." Meanwhile the terrier's lamppost companion, a male basset, inserted this classified ad in the local gazette: "I would like to hear from an attractive female basset. Object: bassinet."

There's a dog in Southampton that just loves to be scrubbed three times every day. His owners aren't absolutely sure of his breed—but they *think* he's a shampoodle.

A prominent banker gave his teen-age daughter, a student at the Actors' Studio, a pedigreed pup for her birthday, warning her that the little dog had not yet been housebroken. Sure enough, an hour later, when he wandered into his daughter's study, he found her contemplating a small puddle in the center of the room. "My pup," she murmured sadly, "runneth over."

There's a kangaroo in the San Diego Zoo who lacks zip. He's frequently discovered out of bounds.

A very large yak next door to the kangaroo is an amiable beast, who wakes up at six every morning and trumpets for his breakfast. San Diego newshawk Don Freeman covered the animal's activities one day, and began his story: "Mighty Yak Arose."

A Kentucky horse breeder named Schubert invariably has his young colts bottle-fed after they're three days old. He knows that a foal and his mummy are soon parted.

What's more:

> Schubert had a horse named Sarah.
> He drove her to a big parade,
> And all the time the band was playing
> Schubert's Sarah neighed.

A great horse, favorite for the Kentucky Derby, found itself domiciled in a Louisville stable between two rather stolid steeds who weren't able to converse intelligently on any subject for more than three minutes. The great horse gave up after several vain attempts, neighing disgustedly to a trainer, "I'm stalling between two fools."

In a workout, this same noble steed ran into one horse that addressed him by name. Obviously puzzled, he confessed, "I can't remember your mane, but your pace is familiar."

Pun addict J. P. Haymart of Lake Como, Florida, who obviously will stop at nothing, relays the dilemma of a neighboring farmer who had to cope with this problem: birds persisted in building nests in his favorite horse's mane. A vet finally told him to try putting yeast in the horse's mane, promising that the birds would then up and fly away. And they did, too. All of which proves, gloats J. P. Haymart, that yeast is yeast, nest is nest, and never the mane shall tweet.

There once was a tolerant cow who stood for absolutely

anything her favorite bull tried to get away with. She reasoned, "To err is human, to forgive bovine." Obviously, this cow needed analysis badly. She had a fodder complex, though everything he told her went in one ear and out the udder. Furthermore, she loved to imbibe ink and always mooed indigo.

When Pat O'Flaherty, having had several beakers of beer too many, swallowed a live rabbit by mistake, Mrs. O'Flaherty lost no time in filling the bathtub with very hot water, throwing Mr. O'F. therein, and declaring, "I'm going to scrub your miserable hide until you cough up that poor little rabbit."

The song that she sang while performing this operation was, of course, "I'm Gonna Wash That Hare Right Out of My Man."

Mary had a swarm of bees,
And they to save their lives
Went everywhere that Mary went,
'Cause Mary had the hives.

Louis Ginsberg of Paterson, New Jersey, is a man who keeps his eyes open. In one day, he spotted a farmer who fell into his well and almost kicked the bucket and a stuffy taxidermist who gave his pet parrot mounting apprehension.

It was one of those nights not fit for man or beast, but a hardhearted father sent his son out to herd the sheep with nothing but an old flickering lamp to guide him. A few hours later, the father found his son fast asleep under a tree, with the lamp extinguished, and awakened him with a solid kick in the rear. Rubbing himself in the appropriate place, the son complained, "It was so cold and dark when my lamp blew out that I surrendered to Morpheus. Do give me a new wick for my lamp." "Nay, nay," his father rebuked him, "and know you this, you sleepyhead. There is no wick for the rested."

FISH STORY

The prettiest she-fish in the whole aquarium was Bess Porgy. Young John Haddock's gills fluttered with suppressed poisson every time she, and her chubby friend Mazie Angelfish slithered down the pike. To kipper in comfort was his consuming obsession.

Trouble loomed, however, when the two girls worked out a sister act and opened at the Globe under the management of Salmon & Schuster. An interested member of the audience was Rufus Goldfish, who sat in the second roe (he was slightly hard of herring) and viewed the performance with a sardinic smile. "Confidentially," he told a grouper friends later, "the girls' act smelt, but they're pretty cute tricks. I found the one who was barracuda."

John Haddock's sole shriveled at these words. "Only an act of cod will keep my Bess out of his clutches," he muttered shadly. Mazie Angelfish tried to rally him. "Don't be blue," she counseled. "You are no common weakfish.

You are a Haddock. Remember Dorothy Vernon of Haddock Hall. Get in there and put that bass sailfish old flounder t'rout!"

John squared what passes for shoulders in a fish. "Thanks, Mazie," he spluttered. "By gum and bivalve, I'll get out of this pickerel yet. If that shrimp expects to mackerel have me to reckon with!"

Suiting the action to the words, he knocked his rival off his perch so effishently that poor Mr. Goldfish whaled for the carps—and a sturgeon to get the bones out of his mouth.

"I did it on porpoise," cried the exultant John Haddock, clasping Bess, who looked prettier than Marlin Dietrich, to his slippery chest.

It was all such a shark to Mr. Goldfish that he's been eel to this very day.

The Haddocks had a tarpon time of it ever after.

FINNY

A wise old crow perched himself firmly on a telephone wire. He wanted to make a long-distance caw.

A resourceful Floridian not only harbored four playful porpoises in a pool behind his house, but discovered a way to keep them alive forever. All he had to do was feed them sea gulls.

So he ventured out in Biscayne Bay and trapped a quantity of gulls. When he tried to re-enter his house, however, he found his way blocked by a peace-loving, toothless old lion who had escaped from the zoo and was stretched clear across the doorway. As our intrepid hero jumped over the dormant beast, a posse of game wardens burst from the surrounding shrubbery and took him into custody.

The charge: Transporting gulls across a staid lion for immortal porpoises. (And that, ladies and gentlemen, is a QUINTUPLE pun!)

3

WORDS ON PLAYS...
Puns About Show Business

Two of the
best-loved men in the theatre were Russel Crouse and
Howard Lindsay. Virtually inseparable in their latter years,
they co-authored such smash hits as "Life with Father" and
"The Sound of Music." Crouse also was a dedicated
punster. Once he startled Lindsay by suddenly appearing
onstage at a matinée of "Life with Father" in the tiny role
of consulting physician. He explained later, "I just wanted
to see if there was a doctor in the Crouse."

Another time, at a sidewalk café in Paris, his wife ordered
a Martini, but Crouse asked only for a glass of water. Then
he signaled for a second round. As he put it to the startled
waiter, "Mrs. Crouse wants another Martini and I'll have
a little more of the Seine."

A Crouse creation of which he was particularly fond (he
said he wrote it on a ride to Punsylvania) involved the Sun-

day-evening opening of a Broadway play starring that glamorous queen of the "silents," Gloria Swanson. While the star was frugally proceeding to the theatre by subway, however, the system broke down, and Miss S. was stranded three miles north of Times Square, necessitating a postponement of the première to the following evening.

The name of this poignant tale, naturally, was "Sick Transit Gloria Monday."

When Ed Wynn was playing the role of a waiter years ago in "Manhattan Mary," a customer demanded lamb chops au gratin. Wynn shouted to the kitchen, "Cheese it, the chops!"

Gypsy Rose Lee was playing a sketch in an old musical revue that called for the property man to ring a deep gong offstage at a certain point in the proceedings. One day the property man misplaced his gong, and in desperation shook a little dinner bell he found on the shelf. The unexpected silvery tinkle caused Miss Lee to burst out laughing, and the punch line of the sketch was lost as a consequence.

When she returned to the wings, she demanded that the property man be fired forthwith. The stage manager, who had been out having a beer while the act was in progress, asked the cause of her ire. Gypsy explained, "He ain't done right by our knell."

It was Walter Winchell who declared that he always praised the first show of a new theatrical season. "Who am I," he asked, "to stone the first cast?"

A Broadway publicity man bought a new electric typewriter and crawled under the desk with the extension cord to plug it in. A client caught him in the act. "You press agents!" he chortled. "Always looking for a plug."

Erudite critic Walter Kerr likes to pun as much as the next fellow. He found on the breakfast table one morning a misaddressed invitation to a dinner that had been held four nights previous. "Well," he commented, tossing the outdated invitation over to his wife, Jean, "there's one fête accompli!"

There was a shapely chorine in the musical, "How Now, Dow Jones," who confessed to a sentimental attachment for a real-life sixty-year-old banker in Wall Street. "Every time he calls," she admitted, "I get chinchillas running up and down my spine."

Mike Douglas, speculating on how flop theatrical ventures first became known as "turkeys," suggests that it may be because so many of them are produced for a poultry sum. (Mike adds that October 1st every year is the day real turkeys start counting how many chopping days there are to Thanksgiving.)

A hard-luck actor who appeared in one colossal disaster after another finally got a break. A broken leg, to be exact. A cruel contemporary pointed out that it's the first time in his career the poor fellow's been in the same cast for more than a week.

Sir James Barrie took his occasional failures philosophically. "Some of my plays pan out," he explained, "some peter out."

Composer-singer Rod McCuen announced that he had an important café date in Kansas City the following Monday. "Better leave Saturday," urged Peter Lind Hayes. "Remember that everything's up two dates in Kansas City."

A singing star's newest recording, for reasons unknown, laid a great big egg. A philosopher at heart, the star tossed off the failure with "R.C.A. tells me I have a slipped disc!"

A novelty act in the Ringling Brothers Circus involves a specialty by an authentic whirling dervish. One day during the circus's Manhattan engagement, an uncommonly handsome damsel picked up this dervish and took him for a row (a Harper & Row?) on the lake in Central Park.

Suddenly the boat tilted, and the frightened damsel quavered to her companion, "I'm afraid I've lost my oar, Derv."

A duo of agile stripteasers named Lola and Beth were cavorting before an all-male audience of art lovers when Lola noticed that the G-string Beth was pleased to call her costume was slipping precariously. A poetry devotee to the core, Lola whispered urgently, "Oh, Beth, where is thy string?"

Just bare with me, and they'll think it's part of the act.

Asked why she was about to embark upon the stormy seas of matrimony for the fifth time in nine years, a still-popular movie queen of the thirties explained, "I guess I'm a sucker for a rite."

A luscious Italian starlet got her big chance in a new multimillion-dollar film spectacle. Unfortunately it was shot in Japan, and after five solid months in Tokyo, where she couldn't speak one word of the language, or eat the native raw fish without getting sick, she confessed to her director that each day made her miss her home in Rome more desperately. "I can't even drink the water here," she complained. "Next time you have to come here from Rome," he suggested, "put a Tiber in your tank."

A Hollywood great lover, who's around the bend but won't admit it, has taken a villa in Aix-les-Bains for the season. "It figures," commented a snide ex-ladylove. "Ham in Aix."

Charlie Kiser is urging old film star George Raft to publish a collection of the funny stories he has picked up over the years. He wants him to call it "The Japes of Raft." He also would like to present Raft with a puppy—so it can hitch its waggin' to a star.

They are trying to catch up with the rash scenario specialist who was observed speaking one evening to those two lovely stars, Maureen O'Sullivan and Maureen O'Hara, and afterward explained glibly, "I heard a funny story today—and I've been telling it to the Maureens."

A dashing movie hero, delight of a million squealing sixteen-year-olds, was told by his studio head, "It's time you played a different kind of role. For your next picture we're casting you as a miner." The hero announced, firmly, "Nothing doing. The last one I met cost me fifty thousand dollars."

A magician and his wife, whom he was wont to saw in half as the climax of the act, retired after a full twenty years on the vaudeville circuit, and opened a dairy outside Los Angeles. The sign over the doorway reads, "Milk sold here by the half gal."

Russell Austin is authority for the tale concerning three young actors named Tom, Fred, and Cec who decided to do the jousting scene from *Don Quixote* for a local TV show. "I'll play the title role," proposed Tom. "Fred can portray Sancho Panza, and Cecil B. De Mille."

Outside the theatre in which the "What's My Line" program used to be televised, panel moderator John Charles Daly was accustomed to pause each Sunday evening to pat traffic cop O'Reilly's horse Brownie and feed it a doughnut. That horse sure loved doughnuts! Came one Sunday, however, when the horse not only refused Daly's doughnut but took a sizable nip out of Daly's left forearm. "What's wrong with Brownie this evening, O'Reilly?" asked the puzzled Daly. To which O'Reilly replied, "Oh, this isn't Brownie, Mr. D. This is a horse of a different cruller."

4

...AND PLAYS ON WORDS
Puns About Semantics

THE GAME OF FITTING
odd words into unlikely sentences is a favorite among truly
dedicated pun-dits. Here are a few favored examples:

APOCRYPHAL: "Hippety-hop to the corner shop for apocryphal of candy."

BOLL WEEVIL: After the boll weevil all go home.

CADILLAC: A Cadillac mean if you pull its tail.

EUPHEMISM: Euphemism and I'm fer youse'm.

LOQUACIOUS: She bumped into me and I told her to
loquacious going.

MACHIAVELLI: I know a tailor who will Machiavelli good
pair of pants for thirty dollars.

MERETRICIOUS: Here's wishing you a meretricious and a
happy New Year.

SOVIET: Dinner was announced, Soviet.

Victor Borge, always interested in semantics, is off on an inflationary binge of late. He's changed "wonderful" to "twoderful," "create" to "crenine," and "forever" to "fivever." He concludes, with a wave of his hand, "And so fifth and so fifth!"

When a Philadelphia shirtmaker offered monetary rewards to people who could dream up new names for "dark blue," "light brown," and other stock colors, some lulus came in from inspired applicants. A few of them: gang green, forever amber, sick bay, hash brown, dorian gray, hi-yo silver, statutory grape, and unpredictable fuchsia.

Remember that once very popular word game called "Fractured French"? Here are a few last-minute nominations by Gary Stevens:

L'ESCARGOT: Let's travel by auto.

DEBUSSY: The maid says they're busy.

DE GAULLE: Some nerve!

DAUPHIN: A fan made of deerskin.

And if you'd like to add some "Splintered Spanish," Mrs. R. A. Henry suggests the following:

Y COMO NO!: Let's listen to Eddie Fisher.

MUCHAS GRACIAS: The lawn needs mowing.

LA SOPA ES FRÍA: Sample box of soap.

ESTOY LISTO: Santa Claus's notebook.

ESO SÍ: Fill 'er up.

LO SIENTO: Cheap perfume.

AL CIUDAD: So long, Pop.

"One reads," notes Bernice Kite, "how lawyers are sometimes disbarred and ministers defrocked." "Would it not be in line," she continues, "if those of us in other walks of life should have equally magnificent terms for getting fired? Far Eastern diplomats, for instance, might be Disoriented, electricians Delighted, cashiers Distilled, equestrians Dismounted, piano tuners Unstrung, mediums Dispirited, cowboys Deranged, guides Detoured, statisticians Disfigured, and teachers Degraded."

By now I'm sure you have the idea.

Here is a list of commands from Jerome Beatty, Jr., who sounds as though he comes from Missouri:

Show me a manhole at a street intersection and I'll show you a connoisseur.

Show me a man who's afraid of Christmas and I'll show you a Noël Coward.

Show me an arrogant insect and I'll show you a cocky roach.

Show me Mohammed Ali's safe-deposit box and I'll show you Cassius' Cash Can.

Show me a squirrel's home and I'll show you a nutcracker's suite.

Mr. Beatty escapes pun-ishment by adding:

Show me a woman who gets down on her hands and knees and I'll show you a woman who's searching for her contact lenses.

Collectors of unusual names have come up with a bumper crop in recent days. A few prize dillies: Xavier

Greenstamps, Sonia Papermoon, Bertha D. Blues, Amanda B. Reckoned-With, Carmen Denominator, and Tyrone Shoelaces.

Dr. Presume?
Dr. Livingstone I. Presume?

Jim Marshall swears that these citizens actually EXIST:
Hans R. Dirty, Jr.: Goan, Wash.
Quoth D. Raven: Never, Mo.
G. Therza Mighty: Pretty, Miss.
Ide Lamy: Down, N. D.
Lettice Finder: Shady, Del.
I. M. Phelin: Slightly, Ill.
Wish I. Newther: Reese, N. Y.
C. U. Sunday: Early, Mass.
Will U. Raider: Cookie, Ga.

Which reminds me that Never-Say-Die Charlie Rice is trying valiantly to revive that old "Knock, knock" fad with the following revolting nominations:

1. Knock, knock. This is Miss Cloud. Which Miss Cloud? Theresa Cloud.
2. This is Mrs. Warner-Cracker. Mrs. Polly Warner-Cracker.
3. This is Mr. Buggy. Mr. Orson Buggy.
4. This is Mr. Rainbows. Mr. Always Jason Rainbows.
5. This is Miss Ruin. Miss Rhoda Ruin.
6. This is Mr. Roome-Ohnley. Mr. Stanton Roome-Ohnley.
7. This is Mr. Deggs. Mr. Hammond Deggs.
8. This is Miss Gettit. Miss Carmen Gettit.
9. This is Mr. Pepper. Mr. Sultan Pepper.
10. This is Mrs. Highwater. Mrs. Helen Highwater.
11. This is Mr. Peace. Mr. Warren Peace.
12. This is Miss Vanation. Miss Bertha Vanation.

Warning: It's hard to put a stop to this sort of thing once you let it get rolling again!

5
SIGN LANGUAGE
Puns in Signs

In an Atlantic City linen shop: "Luxurious Bath Towels for the Whole Damp Family."

At a tire headquarters: "We Skid You Not."

In a butcher shop: "Honest Scales. No Two Weighs About It."

Outside a nudist camp: "Come in Where the Peeling Is Mutual."

In a doctor's anteroom: "Small Fevers Gratefully Received."

In the window of a brassière emporium: "This Is the Real Decoy."

Tied to a cageful of canaries in a pet shop: "For Sale. Cheep."

Over a Penn Central drugstore entrance: "Medicine Square Garden."

Over the chef's table in a fish-house kitchen: "Chief lobstertrician."

At a seaside gift shop: "Buy Your Girl a Bikini and See Her Beam with Delight."

6

DAFFYNITIONS
By Webster? Noah! Noah!

ALASKA: A prelude to "No."

ALIMONY: The fee a woman charges for name-dropping.

ALOHA: A Pullman berth.

AUCTION: A gyp off the old block.

BEAUTY CONTEST: A lass roundup.

BIGAMIST: An Italian fog.

BULLDOZING: Falling asleep during a political speech.

CAMELOT: A place where they park camels.

COMIC RELIEF: When the Life of the Party goes home.

DENIAL: A river in Egypt.

DISBAR: As distinguished from some other bar.

DOGMA: A puppy's mother.

EGOTIST: A man who's always me-deep in conversation.

EXCHEQUER: A retired supermarket employee.

FLATTERY: An apartment house.

GAMBIT: Bitten in the leg.

GIGOLO: A fee-male.

GUILLOTINE: A French chopping center.

HANGOVER: The wrath of grapes.

HATE ORGANIZATIONS: Sour groups.

HYPOTHENUSE: The washroom upstairs is occupied.

IGLOO: An icicle built for two.

INCONGRUOUS: Where the laws are made.

JACKET BLURB: Fable of contents.

LAMB STEW: Much ado about mutton.

MINISKIRT: Hemme fatale.

MOLASSES: Additional girls.

PASTEURIZE: Something you see moving.

POLYGON: A dead parrot.

RAMSHACKLE: A chain used to tie up a he-goat.

SCHNAPPS: Tries to bite you.

SNEEZING: Much achoo about nothing.

SPECIMEN: An Italian astronaut.

SUNBATHER: A fry in the ointment.

TEUTONIC: Not enough gin.

VIOLIN: A very bad hotel.

WOLF: A character who knows all the ankles.

AND

SYNTAX: What the compiler of a treasury like this ought to be required to pay his readers!

7

OPUNING OF THE GATES
Puns about Children
and Their Education

Mr. Ritchie
had just supervised the putting down of a fine new concrete walk outside his villa, and was outraged when he
caught his three children pressing their hands and footprints into the still-wet concrete. He walloped the three of
them until they howled for mercy. "You brute," chided his
wife. "Don't you love your children at all?" Replied Mr.
Ritchie, "In the abstract, yes, but not in the concrete!"

Mrs. Weidman was interviewing a new nurse, and asked
why she had left her last post. "I didn't like the setup,"
the nurse said frankly. "The child was backward, and the
father was forward."

A pre-kindergarten kid in the Bronx explained to the
playground supervisor that her mother "tapped for a
living." "Well, well, a tap dancer," nodded the supervisor.
"And where does your mother tap?"
Explained the youngster, "On her tapwratter."

In the boundless ocean, notes Vera Lawrence, a father drop and a mother drop determined to teach their young offspring how to be a responsible part of the sea. After a month of intensive training, the father drop observed his son's antics with satisfaction.

He then announced to the mother drop, "I do believe we've taught Junior everything he has to know. I hereby declare him fit to be tide."

Suzy Smith put on her skates, upon the ice to frisk.
Her friends thought she was slightly nuts her little *.

Snow White, in a clicking mood one day, used an entire roll of film to record the antics of the seven little dwarfs. Then she mailed the roll to Rochester to be developed. The song she warbled while she awaited delivery was, of course, "Some Day My Prints Will Come."

At dinner one evening, little Willie upset the soup bowl. Then his older brother Max overturned a dishful of stewed tomatoes. Then sister Mae's slab of roast beef slid off the plate onto her newly laundered frock. Finally, Pop Willett overturned a whole platter of ice cream covered with chocolate sauce. "Congratulations, Pop," exclaimed the by now thoroughly exasperated Mrs. Willett. "You've won the spilling bee."

A whole family was caught in a small boat during a sudden storm off the shores of Florida, but towed to safety in Fort Lauderdale by the ever-alert U.S. Coast Guard. "I always knew God would take care of us," said the composed five-year-old daughter of the boatowner after the family got home. "I like to hear you say that," beamed the mother. "Always remember that God is in His heaven watching over us." "Oh, I wasn't talking about THAT God," the five-year-old interrupted. "I was talking about the COAST God."

A certain Mr. Chan who collected teakwood miniatures as a hobby began to notice that they were disappearing, one by one, in the dead of night. Furthermore, muddy footprints on the floor seemed to indicate that the culprit was a small, barefoot boy.

Determined to put an end to all this, Mr. Chan hid himself in the corner of his shop one night. His vigil was rewarded. In came the thief—and it turned out to be a black bear, who promptly started loading up with teakwood. A peculiar feature of this bear was that instead of claws, he had the feet of a little boy.

What could be more natural under the circumstances than the agonized cry from the victim: "Hey, there! Where do you think you're going, oh boy-foot bear with teaks of Chan?"

A twelve-year-old lad was a persistent and dedicated collector of postage stamps—until the kid next door bought an album, too, and began a collection of his own. "He buys every stamp I do," the twelve-year-old complained to his father, "and has taken all the fun out of it for me. I'm quitting." "Don't be a fool, my boy," counseled the father.

"Remember the old adage: Imitation is the sincerest form of philately."

Grandma Heimerdinger sent her favorite grandson a handsome new shirt for his birthday. Unfortunately, it had a size 14 collar and the boy had a size 16 neck. He dutifully wrote her: "Dear Grammy: Thanks heaps. I'd write more—but I'm all choked up."

The ten-year-old son of the richest, most humorless codger in town was a first-rate, four-star, all-American cheat, but the teacher hesitated to snitch on him to the old man. Finally, she compromised on this note: "Judging by his recent written exams, your son is forging his way continuously ahead."

You must have heard about the darling little girl in Puerto Rico named Carmen Cohen. Her father, who made slacks and blazers for the tourists, called her by her last name, Cohen. Her mother, who made the tourists, naturally called her Carmen. So by the time she was ten, the unfortunate kid hardly knew whether she was Carmen or Cohen.

What happens, demands Arthur Madsen, to teachers who retire? They lose their principals. And to principals who retire? They lose their faculties. And to professional basketball players who retire? Nothing. They just go on dribbling.

The instructor of a Freshman English course ordered his

students to write a paper about folks in high society. One co-ed's paper began with a bang: "The Duchess of Dowdy was descending a staircase in the palace when she tripped, fell, and lay prostitute on the floor." The instructor circled the incorrect word and penciled this comment in the margin: "Dear Miss Sherwood: You must learn to distinguish between a fallen woman and one who has merely temporarily lost her balance."

Mourned a once-highflying Senior at Williams: "Last month my tailor told me I could have no more cuffs on my pants. Now he says I can have no more pants on the cuff."

Up at Hanover there's a Dartmouth biologist experimenting with changing the behavior patterns of rodents. Asked to give details of the work he's doing, he's fond of explaining, "I pull habits out of rats."

A student at Boston University wavered for some time before a career as a barber or life as a proctologist. He ultimately flipped a coin to see how it came up: heads or tails.

Appreciative students at Stanford have planted a cluster of trees in honor of their math wizard, Pat Suppes. All the trees have square roots.

Very much against his wishes, Dr. Suppes's classroom was recently remodeled. Ever since, he's been mooning about, sighing for the good old dais.

CAMPUS CUTUPS . . .

From U.C.L.A.:

A Romeo returned from a cotillion in Santa Barbara sporting a black eye and badly swollen lip. "Run into a door at the party?" he was asked. "No," replied the Romeo ruefully. "I was struck by the beauty of the place."

From U. of Texas:

Bride-to-be: Have you made any reservations for our honeymoon, darling?

Bridegroom-to-be: Certainly not—and I hope you haven't, either!

From Williams:

Lawyer: Did you say the plaintiff was shot in the woods, Doctor?

Doctor: I did not. I said he was shot in the lumbar region.

From Rutgers:

Real-estate man: Would you like to see a model home?

Rutgers Senior: I sure would. What time does she quit work?

Revived at V.P.I.:

A hillbilly ventured into a drugstore and asked for a can of talcum. The clerk asked, "Mennen's?" The hillbilly answered, "No, Wimmen's." The clerk asked, "Do you want it scented?" The hillbilly answered, "No, I'll take it with me."

From Brown:

A proper Bostonian went to Las Vegas for a change and a rest. The hotel maids got the change and the croupiers got the rest.

From Vanderbilt:

Six months after he had been appointed dogcatcher, Pa Trimblett hadn't reported once for work. His alibi: "I ain't found out yet what I'm supposed to catch them at!"

From Columbia:

Soph: Why were you hanging around so long at that steamroller accident?

Frosh: I was just scraping up an acquaintance.

From Johns Hopkins:

Four ghosts were playing poker when there was a knock on the door. "Who is it?" they asked. "Rigor Mortis" was the chilling reply. "May I set in?"

In the days when George S. Kaufman and Moss Hart were collaborating on play hits, George's daughter Anne interrupted one time to report that her best friend had deserted Vassar to run off with a young producer. "Ah," observed Kaufman. "She's put the heart before the course!"

(It was Kaufman, too, who pointed out that one man's meat is another man's poisson.)

A classic story in literary circles concerns the three English professors who, returning to the campus, encountered a pushy group of young ladies who obviously were no better than they should be. Evading them gracefully, one professor—a Shakespearean scholar—chuckled, "What might one call such a congregation? A flourish of strumpets?" The second professor, whose specialty was Anthony Trollope, understandably preferred "a chapter of trollops." But the winner was the third and youngest professor's nomination, "an anthology of pros."

8

LOVE AND MARRIAGE
Puns About Sex

Elders of the Pilgrim colony of Massachusetts had good cause to remember the morning their hitherto impeccable Mr. Standish got fresh with a fair young maiden. It was from this moment forward that Mr. Standish was always referred to by Pilgrims in the know as "Naughtical Myles."

A society belle decided to give a new beau from Harvard the air. He turned out to be a little bit too rough around the hedges.

In *One Man's Gold Rush*, a volume of remarkable photographs of the Klondike boom in 1900, Murray Morgan, who contributes the text, tells of the wild-and-woolly dance hall in Dawson, presided over by a Mae Westian amazon known as Diamond-Tooth Gertie. Star boarder of this élite retreat was a lady named Gad Wilson, who explained at regular intervals, "My ma told me to be a good girl and pick nice clean friends—and I leave it to you, don't I pick 'em clean?"

Susie Shnickelputz was unanimously voted the most popular girl in school by the graduating male half of the senior class. They weighed her in the balance and found her wanton.

An overdressed character, who labored under the erroneous impression that women found him irresistible, was trying hard to make time with the curvaceous operator of an elevator in a skycraper. As they ascended to the fiftieth floor, he smiled a toothy smile and murmured, "I bet all these stops and starts get you pretty worn out." "It isn't the stops and starts that get on my nerves," she snapped. "It's the jerks."

A handsome young couple was waltzing dreamily under the stars in Barbados. The girl gazed fondly at her partner and whispered, "You're the kind of man I feel I can trust." "Really?" replied the boy soulfully. "Say, we must have met someplace before. Your faith seems familiar."

Traveling salesman: Aren't you the pretty youngster who used to shrink from my embrace?
Farmer's daughter: I don't recoil now.

A jealous broker asked his partner, "Who was that luscious little blonde I saw you outwit last night?"

It's the theory of Jess Birnbaum, of *Time* magazine, that women with bad legs should stick to long skirts because they cover a multitude of shins.
It's not the initial skirt length, Jess, it's the upcreep.

An American lad in Paris found a cute chick who struck his fancy, and just before flying back to Stanford he gave her a present which he deemed very ample under the circumstances. She, obviously, did not—but did manage a listless "merci." The Stanford lad—majoring in Shakespeare, no doubt—shook his head sadly and observed, "The quality of your 'merci' is strained."

Gary Nordell tells of a very busy Air Force cadet who managed to get himself engaged to two beautiful girls at the same time: one named Edith, in California, and the other named Kate, in Texas. Unfortunately for the cadet, the two girls met at a beauty contest, discovered their boy friend's duplicity, and confronted him with an ultimatum: "Out of our lives, you rascal. We'll teach you that you can't have your Kate and Edith, too."

The month of June, rhapsodizes Ogden Nash, is the time when "Ladies grow loony and gentlemen loonier;/This year's June is next year's Junior."

Chants happy bachelor John Wycherly:

> "A bachelor is a cagey guy
> And has a load of fun:
> He sizes all the cuties up
> And never Mrs. one."

Less than a month ago, a domineering he-man married a mere wisp of a girl. He's back from his honeymoon a chastened groom. He's become aware of the will of the wisp.

Stanley Compton, a marriage counselor, writes that in the course of his studies he's encountered a confused bride who put all her eggs in one biscuit, a couple who haven't even talked to each other since their honeymoon (a clear case of delight that failed), and a young husband with an inferiority complex who insisted that he was just a little pebble on the beach. "If you wish to save your marriage," Counselor Compton told him, "You'd better be a little boulder."

Reporter to TV star: Am I correct, sir, in my belief that your new bride has been married five times and that you have been married twice?

TV star: Yes, she's three chumps ahead of me.

An impetuous young husband deliberately threw three pairs of trousers into the furnace one Sunday, then told his wife, "No longer can you accuse me of being a stick-in-the-mud, unwilling to take a chance. I have just burned my breeches behind me."

An unfortunate husband in Hackensack socked his wife with a bowl of Jello. She emerged unscathed if messy, then had him arrested for carrying a congealed weapon.

It was a different story in Lincoln, where a Nebraska bride let her groom have one on his noggin with a heavy glass pitcher. "There's one lady," pointed out a sympathetic boarder, "who conks to stupor."

Lament by L. Kleist:

> The bank sent our statement this morning.
> The sheet was a sight of great awe.
> Its figures and mine might have balanced,
> But my wife was too quick on the draw!

Mrs. O'Brien reported to Mr. O'Brien: "It says in the paper that a man on the next block throttled his mother-in-law yesterday." "Hmm," mused Mr. O'B., who always favored a little pun in bed, "sounds to me like a practical choker."

"Your wife never stops talking. How on earth can you stand it?" marveled a henpecked husband's luncheon guest. "I know," sighed the resigned husband. "I've given that woman the best ears of my life."

Joey Adams defines alimony as "the billing without the cooing."

"I'm afraid my poor wife can never have a child," sighed a frustrated husband. "Inconceivable, eh?" asked a friend. "No, I mean unbearable," said the husband. "Impregnable," amended the friend.

A young childless wife named Faith adopted a baby but found it more troublesome than she had bargained for and sought to return to it the agency where she had found it. This displeased her husband, on the road for a sales trip, so he hastily wired her, "KEEP THE BABY, FAITH."

9

HOT CROSS PUNS
Puns About Food and Drink

PROUD AS PHILADELPHIANS
are of William Penn, few know that he boasted a couple
of aunts named Natalie and Ellie who were past mistresses
in the art of whipping up a mince pie or an apple strudel.
When Quakertown bakers formed a combine and tripled
the price of their pastries overnight, Aunt Natalie and Aunt
Ellie decided to teach the greedy fellows a lesson. They put
their delectable concoctions on the market at bare cost—
and then proceeded to reduce the price five cents a day.

In no time, the good citizens of Quakertown were dis-
cussing only one topic: the pie rates of Penn's aunts.

Bob Satre, indefatigable researcher of American Revolu-
tion data, claims that a British soldier, on the eve of the
Battle of White Plains, tripped while he was raiding a well-
stocked chicken coop. He fell heavily to the ground, where
he was pinned down by a belligerent Rhode Island Red

until the Chinese cook employed by the American owners burst upon the scene. "Ho, ho," chuckled the Chinese cook, "chicken catch a Tory!"

That fine poet and humorist of yesteryear, James Whitcomb Riley, once was told by his Washington landlady about an unfortunate cook in the neighborhood who that day had fallen asleep over her red-hot stove and burned to death. Gravely and unhesitatingly, Riley pronounced the epitaph "Well done, good and faithful servant."

Robert Perloff, of West Lafayette, Indiana, wants you to know how pitted prunes came into being. It seems the prune family became concerned over the fact that people were passing them by because they resented having to remove and dispose of the pits, so they decided they would henceforth be pitted—figuring that it's better to be pitted than scorned.

A Richmond baker has perfected a new variety of doughnut. He calls it the "Phyfe." Soon, he hopes, every lover of antiques will be dunking Phyfes.

Robert Orben's wife went on a chopped-meat binge one week. On Monday she served him hamburger, on Tuesday meat loaf, Wednesday tartar steak, and Thursday meatballs. On Friday morning, he collared her in the kitchen and inquired resignedly, "How now, ground cow?"

Sam Himmell was trying to explain to a waiter in a

chop-suey emporium a succulent dish he once had been served in Hong Kong. "I'm sure it was some kind of duck," recalled Sam, "but at the same time it tasted like fish." "Ah, yes," beamed the waiter. "Hadduck!"

A famous Washington newspaperman was dining at Galatoire's, in the old French quarter of New Orleans, and raved over the trout Marguery. He summoned the proprietor and said, "I'd like to have the recipe for this dish." The proprietor smiled and answered suavely, "I'm sorry, sir, but we have the same policy here as you journalists. We never reveal our sauce."

The wife of a distinguished classical scholar planned a birthday cake for him decorated with quotations from the Greek poets. Unfortunately, it tasted terrible—proving once more that we can't have archaic and eat it, too.

They're trying to persuade J. Paul Getty, reputedly the richest man in the world, to open an Italian restaurant. They've got a name picked out for it, too: "Spa Getty."

Meanwhile, they're building a snack bar next to the new atom smasher in Weston, Illinois. This one will be called "The Fission Chips."

Have you heard about the cook at a roadside tavern who put a giant firecracker under a platter of pancakes? He had determined to blow his stack.

A cannibal chief's secretary interrupted him at dinner

to tell him he was wanted on the phone. The chief cried angrily, "Stop bothering me. Can't you see I'm in the middle of somebody?"

This chief, incidentally, is quite a devil with the ladies, though he wants only girls who are game. His nine wives have learned what to do with their leftovers. They make chap suey. The chief himself—an Oxford man—is presently anthologizing dog stories confided to him by other cannibal potentates. His book, naturally, will be called *The Golden Bowwow.*

"I would like to reaffirm my belief in Buddha," said Hop Lee May, "but on the other hand there is a great deal to be said for margarine."

Frank Sinatra once engaged a chef freshly imported from Bombay, but after serving the same menu six nights running he was discharged. Explained Sinatra, "This was one poor guy who got fired for favoring curry."

A nearsighted débutante turned up for a soirée very much under the weather. "I can't see," she mourned. "I couldn't put in my contact lenses because my poodle bit me in the eye this afternoon." "What did he do that for?" asked the hostess. "Heaven knows," admitted the débutante. "Probably he felt like having an eyeball before dinner."

A character who identified himself as Joshua Thompson was hauled up in court for making corn liquor in the woods. "Joshua," mused the judge, with the hint of a smile, "are you the Joshua who caused the sun to stand still?" "No, suh," declared the defendant emphatically. "I'se the Joshua that made the moonshine."

An American tourist wandered into a small Hamburg rathskeller and demanded a dry Martini. The waiter looked blank, so the tourist repeated, "Dry Martini!" The waiter shuffled off and came back with three Martinis.

Punster Cousins entertained a Norwegian confrere at a neighborhood pub last week. The Norwegian lifted his drink and said, "Skoal." "Of course it is," said Cousins, nodding. "It's got ice in it."

A forlorn drunk staggered into a funeral parlor and demanded a Scotch-and-soda. When the undertaker explained where he was, the drunk pulled himself together and announced, "O.K., in that case give me a bier."

Despite a violent downpour, Heywood Broun managed to arrive at a banquet only an hour or so late, and was served a beaker of extremely bad wine. Downing it with some distaste, Broun finally philosophized, "Oh, well, any port in a storm."

A restaurant owner who specializes in low-calorie concoctions boasts, "My dishes will take your breadth away." One of this gentleman's waiters, incidentally, spilled a couple of under-fried eggs in a customer's lap the other day.

Quipped the good-natured customer (before socking the waiter in the jaw), "I guess the yolk's on me."

For the grand opening of a super-de-luxe delicatessen in Las Vegas, the proud owner trotted out everything from the customary klieg lights to a pair of famous Ping-Pong champions who played on a table in front of the marquee. Since it was a delicatessen they were advertising, the players substituted pickles for the customary Ping-Pong balls, and the crowd cheered madly as they batted the pickles back and forth across the net. Their exhibition, of course, was advertised as "The Volley of the Dills."

10

PUNNY BUSINESS
Puns About Commerce and High Life

AN ENTERPRISING reporter wangled his way aboard the yacht of billionaire Greek shipowner Aristotle Onassis when it was anchored offshore at Monte Carlo and asked if it was true that he intended marrying a famous opera singer. The billionaire, a punster on the side, evaded the issue by remarking, "That rumor ain't Onassisarily so."

After receiving no less than five urgent requests for contributions "because of an emergency" from the same badly managed home for something or other, an exasperated donor wrote the chairman: "I'll have to ask you to remove my name from your succor list."

A man recently arrived from Napoli approached the floorwalker in a big department store and asked politely, "You tella me, please, where is rest room?"

The floorwalker pointed to the left and answered politely, "Escalator, sir."

"Escalator," echoed the Italian indignantly. "I gotta go now."

"There's one thing about taking dictation from my boss," sighed Mr. Sideman's secretary. "You have to take a lot for grunted."

The boys in the research department at Ford Motors say they haven't decided yet upon a name for that electricity-driven economy car they're working on. How about Con Edsel?

Allen Boretz was at the bedside when the president of the Amicable Loan Company breathed his last. As the doctor drew the sheet over the face of the departed, Boretz heard him murmur, "He has gone to his co-maker."

A favorite yarn at bankers' conventions concerns the president of the Eighteenth National who fell overboard on a seagoing yacht. While his pals frantically sought a life preserver, a sailor shouted, "Hey—can you float alone?" "Of course I can," gasped the floundering banker, "but this is a hell of a time to talk business."

There's a rich old reprobate in the Wall Street sector who still has an eye for the girls. He's generally acknowledged one of the town's greatest natural athletes. He makes every broad jump.

The wife of a newly elected Congressman nagged her husband until he angrily agreed to hornswoggle a job at the Statehouse for her good-for-nothing brother. Said brother declared, "Unless the job is an important one, I won't take it." Retorted the Congressman, "It's important, all right. I'm getting you a post with vital public relations responsibility. Just don't make it public that we're relations."

Senator Ala.: Think we should start a filibuster?
Senator Miss.: Yes, Ah do. It's time we threw our wait around.

"Certain senators owe their popularity to the fact that they have discovered the secret of perpetual emotion."— Angus Fennell.

The promoter of a big flower show in Philadelphia had to postpone the opening because the exhibits couldn't be installed in time. He admitted, "They caught us with our plants down."

(It is entirely possible that this promoter owed his exalted post to strict observance of Franklin P. Adams' famous injunctions: "Take care of the peonies and the dahlias will take care of themselves.")

There's an enterprising lady plumber in Denver named Molly who invented a stainless-steel kitchen sink. Naturally, she's calling it the Unbrownable Molly Sink.

At a church board meeting, the minister dropped a

bombshell by suddenly announcing his resignation. "I have had a call from a larger parish," he explained. The deacons, after recovering from their surprise, wished him well, and one finally asked the question all of them wanted to: "How much are they going to pay you in your new parish?" "Five thousand a year," said the minister. "Wowie!" exclaimed the deacon. "That isn't a call; that's a raise!"

Jack Fuller cites these unfortunates who have taken a lot of pun-ishment:

(1) The mobster at a gangland funeral who observed, "They shouldn't put all those yeggs in one casket"; (2) the baseball pitcher with a sore arm, in the throws of agony; (3) the Madison Avenue account executive who bought himself a sincere-sucker suit; and (4) the firemen who answered a call from a lingerie shop, but found when they arrived that there had been no fire. Their official report read, "Falsie Alarm."

A Reverend Goodenuf in Atlanta asked to speak to a Reverend Nicely in Waco. "And remember," he cautioned the long-distance operator, "this is a parson-to-parson call."

Sign observed outside the farmhouse of the Reverend Silas Beazle: "All Those Wishing a Free Chicken for the Holiday, Apply Within. Our Coop Runneth Over."

Unquestionably, the brawniest and most imposing delegate at a recent U.N. assembly was a seven-foot-two giant from a newly formed African state. "You are a magnificent specimen of mankind," gushed a lady reporter. "What do you eat to keep in such superb condition?" "Beans" was his laconic reply. "Beans!" echoed the unbelieving reporter. "Do you mean soybeans? Navy beans? String beans?" "I do not," snapped the delegate. "I mean HUMAN bein's."

At another U.N. gathering, actress Shelley Winters and a dignified nun walked up to sign the guest register at the same time. Miss Winters, anxious to get the ceremony over with, didn't know she had stepped directly in front of the nun until her companion cautioned her, "Wait till the nun signs, Shelley."

The first astronaut to reach the moon had barely climbed out of his rocket ship when a host of peculiar-looking men descended upon him. They had faces made of green tin with eyes that looked like the headlights of a Manhattan subway train. "Who are you?" gasped the astronaut. "We are the Furries," explained the little men. "This part of the moon is our domain." "Good enough," said the astronaut, with a nod. "Now please take me to your leader." It developed that the leader looked just like all the other Furries —with one additional feature. Out of the top of his head grew a large hypodermic needle. "Wh-what do they call *you?*" stammered the astronaut. "I," answered the leader modestly, "am the Furry with the syringe on top."

11

DRY DOCS
Puns About Medicos
and Hospitals

INTERNATIONAL BEAUTY –
Zsa Zsa Horntoot managed to get some vinegar in her ear
one morning. Now she suffers from pickled hearing.

Pat Harrington was trying to place a call with a long-
distance operator on an evening when he was suffering
with a miserable cold. When he gave the number, the operator asked, "Have you an area code?" "Not at all," Pat
assured her. "It's just my darn laryngitis."

Know why the prettiest nurse at St. Luke's Hospital is
known as "Appendix"? Only the doctors are allowed to take
her out.

A young man in white passed a pretty girl in a Los
Angeles hospital corridor. He cauterize and winked. She
interne winked back. (They were both attending a limping

patient, who kept complaining, "My heel is Achille-ing me.")

The pretty girl, meanwhile, kept tugging constantly at her dress and wiggling uncomfortably. Obviously, she was a chafing dish!

A dental surgeon stood back and shook his head at the young thing in the chair. "My dear," he said, "I don't like to tell you this, but you've got acute pyorrhea." "Never mind that now, Doctor," snapped the young thing. "Just get on with your dentistry."

A rich old coot from Albuquerque fled his hospital bed one spring morning, jetted over to Tangier, and bought himself a harem. He's got delusions of glandeur!

A pun-dit obviously willing to take his life in his hands tells about a patient who confessed to his analyst a strange compulsion to jump out of bed each night and play a jukebox. "Ah ha!" chuckled the analyst. "You obviously are going from bed to Wurlitzer!"

A young psychiatrist, serving his apprenticeship in a huge, ill-equipped state mental institution, fell madly in love with a spectacular blond nurse and proposed matrimony. She stalled for time, however, telling him coyly, "Not yet, my Lochinvar. But come around again when you know how to own your mind business."

Two of Newcastle's finest undertakers, Old Mort Rogers

68

and his brother Dick, are experts at rigging sailing ships on the side. Natives agree that although Dick is a mighty fine shipbuilder, he's not the rigger Mort is. (How awful can a pun BE??)

An up-and-coming young psychiatrist has this slogan adorning his letterhead: "REMEMBER THE MANIA!"

A San Francisco undertaker was sliding a coffin into the hearse on a cold winter's day when it slipped out of his hands, landed on the icy pavement, skidded down a hill, sailed straight through the town drugstore entrance, and slid past the prescription counter. The undertaker came puffing along and implored the apothecary, "For heaven's sake, give me something to stop this coffin."

12

CRIME AND PUN-ISHMENT
Puns About the Law

STATISTICIAN FRANCIS DUFFY opines that when the inheritance taxers, the excise taxers, the surrogates, and the army of lawyers get through settling an estate, the friendless beneficiary doesn't have a legacy to stand on.

There was a bit of a racket along Wabash Avenue in Chicago one afternoon this April. Two automobiles came hurtling out of nowhere, with the occupants wildly shooting at each other with machine guns. The cop at the corner merely yawned and observed to nobody in particular, "Heavens to Betsy! That's the first robin' I've heard this spring!"

A truck belonging to a wholesale perfume distributor was hijacked in New Jersey some weeks ago, and thousands of dollars' worth of expensive toiletries and fragrances went down the drain. The president of the company called the police a few days after the robbery and asked if the crooks had been apprehended. "Not yet," admitted the police chief, "but we're on the scent."

Judge: I'll just fine you ten dollars this time, but if it happens again tomorrow, I'll throw you into jail.

First offender (an inveterate punster): I get it, Your Honor. Fine today, cooler tomorrow.

There's a cop with a sense of humor in Pensacola, Florida. Near an important intersection he's put up a sign reading, "For That Run-Down Feeling, Try Crossing Here Against the Light."

In Charleston, S.C., a perfectly innocent pedestrian,

staring at a lot of shiny new dentures in a shopwindow, was pinched for picking his teeth in public.

A story from the Montpelier sector concerns a quarry owner who was arrested for overcharging. He was taking too much for granite.

Out in Kansas, an unkempt youth was hauled into court for the fourth time—always for the same offense: riding off on somebody else's motor scooter. The judge remarked, "Young man, you are obviously a cycle-path."

One of the most ornate and widely gossiped-about houses of ill repute in the country was invaded by a band of unromantic robbers some nights ago, and all the cash and valuables on the premises were taken. The moral of this sad tale is that too many crooks spoil the brothel.

"So you're a locksmith, eh?" grumbled a judge as he peered over his glasses at a mousy little man cowering before the bench. "Then, pray tell me, what was a locksmith doing in a gambling den when the vice squad made its raid?" Answered the mousy little man, "If it please Your Honor, I was making a bolt for the door."

A police captain, regarded as something of an egghead by subordinates, was shown two sets of fingerprints of a suspected robber. "These can't belong to the same man," objected the captain. "They're whorls apart."

A trusty at a state prison farm routed the warden from his bed, shouting, "There's a character outside attaching an airplane propeller to his old jalopy. I think he's preparing to fly the coupe."

There was a fellow out in Battle Creek, Michigan, whose name was Joe Kissinger. He hated the name Kissinger, so he went to court and changed it to Mackay. Two months later he tired of Mackay and changed it to Johnson. Then he decided he had made another mistake and persuaded the judge to change it to Loomis. By this time, all his friends had begun to ask, "I wonder who's Kissinger now?"

There's a siren in Taiwan who just inherited five million bucks. She's one fortunate Chinese cookie.

Johnny Carson may not care to be reminded of the fact, but in one of his recent engagements in Las Vegas he told of a couple watching TV in bed, the while they munched on Smucker's jam and crackers. For some reason the husband waxed wroth with his bride and smeared Smucker's jam all over her lovely countenance. The next day the unpredictable wife sued the Smucker's Jam Company. It was the first case in the history of the law of a smear-Smucker suit.

13

SOME FOR THE BOOK
Puns About the Literary World

"Don't let the word 'paronomasia' throw you," advises author and columnist John Fuller. "All it means is an old-fashioned pun."

Dr. Fuller thereupon gives a few examples, such as the missionary who was seized by cannibals, tied to a post, and jabbed with daggers so that the savages could drink his blood. After a week he told the chief, "Look, I'm tired of being stuck for the drinks." And the songwriter and some cronies who were held up briefly at the International Bridge at Niagara, and warbled, "Just a cortege small by a waterfall." And the critic who brushed off a particularly sappy romance by a best-selling lady novelist with "Chacun à son goo."

"When my ship comes in," daydreamed a Bryn Mawr Sophomore, "I'm going to buy me a place in the country with lots of chickens, ducks, and seven turkeys." "Why exactly seven turkeys?" her roommate wanted to know.

She explained, "So I can call it 'The House of the Seven Gobbles.'"

Bob McMillen, associate editor of *Farm Journal*, dawdled over a second cup of coffee one Sunday morning reading *The Canterbury Tales*. His father demanded, "What have you got there?" McMillen answered, "Just my cup and Chaucer."

A particularly unkempt and untalented Village poet persisted in submitting his material to a tough editor of a national weekly. The editor finally wrote him, "For heaven's sake, curb your doggerel."

An incurable punster was the late distinguished publisher Ben Huebsch. There was the day, for instance, when Ben announced, "I am going to sneeze." "At whom?" asked his partner, a long-suffering soul named Best. "At-choo," said Ben. And the time he disclosed, "My secretary is in love with fourteen soldiers, but she says it's platoonic." I think you'll agree that he really went too far, though, when he called a friend on the phone and said, "If buttercups are yellow, what color are hiccups?" "I give up," sighed the friend wearily. "Burple," said Ben. They yanked out his phone a few minutes later.

The wife of a pun-drunk novelist, who wisely chooses to remain anonymous, came running to him one day as he brilliantly avoided work on his overdue manuscript. "Dr. Jensen," she reported, "has become a naval surgeon." "Ah," he replied, "what a specialist." "You aren't as gallant as you were when a boy," pouted his wife. "No," said the novelist, "and you aren't as buoyant as you were when a gal." At this moment his Pomeranian barked at him (the dog was a bit of a critic). The man of many words booted the pup and remarked blithely, "I have no intention of letting a Pom de terre me." He then burst into his theme song: "Orange Juice Sorry That I Made You Cry?"

In their youth, humorists Frank Sullivan and Corey Ford shared a fleabag in an inexpensive but faintly disreputable boarding house. Ford named the tiny apartment, "Cloister on the Half Shell." Sullivan referred to himself as "Ford's Ugly Roomer."

John Gunther, author of all those enormously popular *Inside* books, once asked Mr. Sullivan, "What am I going to do when I run out of continents?" Sullivan promptly suggested, "Try incontinence."

The late Oliver Herford once visited a prominent nose and throat specialist, and found himself in the midst of a group of sinus patients who had had their treatments and were pulling themselves together in the waiting room. "They have come to cough," observed Mr. Herford, "but remained to spray."

One bitter winter morning, a lady complained to gentle parodist S. J. Perelman, "It's too cold here in New York." "Go south of the border," advised Perelman. "It may be Chile there today, but it'll be hot tamale."

Louis Untermeyer characterized composers plagiarizing from Debussy as "Debussybodies." Christopher Fry noted that a silver-tongued but opportunistic orator was "coruscating on thin ice." Max Beerbohm declined to be lured into a hike to the summit of a Swiss Alp. "Put me down," he said firmly, "as an anti-climb Max."

When Richard Spong was undergraduate editor of the Dartmouth newspaper, he sent a Freshman cub to cover a wedding some miles outside Hanover. The bride—a Vassar graduate—informed the young reporter loftily, "You may say that when we return from our honeymoon, we will reside at the old manse." The story the Freshman handed in to Spong read, "After their honeymoon, the young couple will dwell at the home of the bride's father."

A novelist confided to friends that he had acquired a hundred hens and wanted names for them. The following were among those suggested: Macduff; Chickov; Eggetha Christie; Henny VIII; Shelley; Gregory Peck; Gizzard of Oz; Himalaya; Pullett Goddard; Fryer Tuck; Ku Klux; Peck and Peck; and the Brooders Karamazov.

A Minnesota doctor named Challman has taken it upon himself to compile a list of "Household Poets," and includes therein, reasonably enough, Burns for the kitchen, Lamb for the dining room, Lovelace for the boudoir, Suckling for the nursery, Seegar for the smoking room, Dryden for the laundry, and out thar in the barn De la Mare.

On the side, Dr. Challman's rounding up some "Occupational Poets." Already corraled are Wordsworth for authors, Donne for bill collectors, Pope for the Catholic clergy, and Longfellow for the basketball crowd.

In *The Vale of Laughter*, latest of Peter De Vries's pun-filled novel successes, he named his hero Joe Sandwich, just so his son could be nicknamed "Ham." One of Ham's projects was a night club especially designed for aging swingers. It was named, of course, "The Slipped Discothèque."

"Writers," notes Ann K. Pipe, "used to be a sickly lot." Proof of the pudding: "Bret had a bad Harte, John a Bunyan, Robert suffered from Burns, Thomas lived in Paine, Graham looked Greene, and Thomas Gray. In fact, only Edward Everett and Thomas could be truly regarded as Hale and Hardy."

In describing what makes the books by Dr. Seuss so fantastically popular with children all over the country (his *The Cat in the Hat* has sold over two million copies), pun-dit Arthur Gordon notes, "He makes Edward Lear and Ogden Gnash his teeth."

Poet Richard Armour suggests a new name for writer's cramp: authoritis. We'll make rheum for it.

Joe Onsrud tells about a Wisconsin trapper who came to town to buy a case of soft drinks and a copy of *Of*

Human Bondage. He left both on a table in a lunchroom and wandered about for a while. When he came back, the book had disappeared. "You having some trouble?" asked the proprietor. "I sure am," answered the trapper. "I've found my pop but I've lost my Maugham!"

Gloria Steinem, one of the loveliest as well as cleverest young journalists in the country, spends much of her spare time on nonsense like the following:

Proverbs:

If Dana Wynter comes, can Spring Byington be far behind?
Hope Hampton springs eternal in the human breast.
Lauren Bacall but few are chosen.
Absence makes the heart grow Fonda.
All that glitters is not Herbert Gold.
A Benny Goodman is hard to find.
Leave Edward Durell Stone unturned.
There's many a slip twixt Irv Kupcinet and Walter Lippmann.

Songs:

Susskind of Fool Am I?
Doris Day, You Are the One
There's a Kitty Hart for Every Light on Broadway

Titles:

Warhol Is Hell

Nevil Shute the Piano Player: He's Doing the Best He
  Can
His Eye Is on Mia Farrow
Fiedler on the Roof
Fly Now, I. M. Pei later.

An English teacher in a suburban school near Chicago
asked his class to list all the books they could recall dealing
with horses—and was mildly surprised when one nymphet
included that old adventure classic *She*. Asked what on
earth this book had to do with horses, the nymphet explained, "Well, for one thing, it's by that famous rider,
Haggard."

An agent submitted a sheaf of essays to a publisher, and
protested bitterly when they were rejected. "You are passing
up a potential genius," he declared. "This man's writing
will be studied in colleges one day." "Stuff and nonsense,"
laughed the editor. "You're just making a Montaigne out
of a molehill."

"I can't tell you how long I have labored on this manuscript," the aspiring writer told the producer, "polishing a
scene here, adding a line there, eliminating scenes, and
adding new characters." "What a pity," said the producer,
handing it back to him. "All work—and no play."

A remarkable character named Alemany has compiled
these literary notes:
1. Mark Twain wrote a book about what his hero would

do when his best friend died. (Huck'll Bury Finn.)

2. Sir Walter Scott wrote about the occupation of the Russian farmer. (Ivan Hoe.)

3. J. D. Salinger wrote what would happen if a husband came home and found his wife in a tub full of whiskey. (Catch Her in the Rye.)

4. And the best seller of them all tells us what the cow said when her gentleman friend was leaving the pasture. ('Bye, Bull.)

Some months ago, the clever and purposeful gents who edit *Time* magazine honored me with a cover story in which they chided me, not without cause, for the horrendous puns I sometimes perpetrate, but then they added fuel to the fire with a couple of beauts of their own. One editor instructed a correspondent in darkest Africa: "Next time some antelopes in Ghana snake in and monkey around with the gnus, lemur know." A book critic called *Peyton Place* a "peeping tome," and another reported that the literary set was "whooping it up in the Malamud salon." *Time* men, too, were the ones who dubbed Adenauer "der Alter Ego" and Khrushchev "the Vulgar Boatman."

The famous if sometimes unintelligible Gertrude Stein was about to cross the Champs-Elysées in Paris one afternoon when she paused to rub a mosquito bite on the back of her neck. Just then an automobile out of control careered down the avenue, missing Gertrude by a matter of seconds —and inches. Miss Stein's companion, Alice B. Toklas, murmured thankfully, "An itch in time saves Stein."

14

NARY A FALSE NOTE
Puns About Music
and Musicians

THERE WAS THE DEVIL
to pay the morning that Baron Shtuffelheim burst unannounced into Ludwig van Beethoven's Vienna studio and found the great composer stretched out in an open coffin on the floor. "Gott in Himmel," stammered Baron Shtuffelheim, "what are you doing in that coffin?" "Heraus!" cried Beethoven querulously. "Can't you see I'm decomposing?"

Then there was the great composer Bach, who, whenever he worked away from home, developed a prodigious appetite. So every time he went on a trip he packed a valise with six sandwiches, three apples, some cheese, and a selection of cookies. This became known as a "Bach's lunch."

And when the great Maestro Toscanini first conducted an all-Bach concert, he pushed his orchestra so fiercely and relentlessly in rehearsal they dubbed him "the Bach Suite Driver."

Hunt Clark has dreamed up a cluster of occupational theme songs I'm sure some readers of this treasury will want to augment. Examples: for outdoor cooks, "The Bastings in Life Are Free"; for alcoholics, "I get a Hic Out of You"; for the nearsighted, "On a Bifocal Built for Two"; for the bearded gentry, "I've Got You Under My Chin."

James Davis, possibly befuddled by conflicting claims of the beer merchants on TV, submits a "Brewery Hop Parade" that includes "My Beer Bist Du Schoen," "Keg of My Heart," "Brews in the Night," and "Foam on the Range." Cask me another!

Abel Green, top banana at *Variety*, bible of show biz, detects a distinct French influence in Tin Pan Alley. Examples: "Matisse This Thing Called Love?" "I'm Always Chasing Rimbauds," "When Derain Goes Pitter-Patter," "Picasso Love You," and "Rouault, Rouault, Rouault Your

Boat." Of course, Spain can always counter with "Hello, Dali."

Goddard Lieberson, boss man of C.B.S. Records, whiles away spare moments by insinuating people's names into old song titles. A few of his zanier inspirations: "When the Saints Come Ho Chi Minh"; "I Want a Girl Just Like the Girl That Marat Dear Old Sade"; "It Happened at Martha Raye a Long Time Ago."

Sad was the predicament of the man who played the French horn for a famous civic orchestra one season. In the middle of the opening symphony, his toupee fell into his instrument. He spent the rest of the evening blowing his top.

The great Artur Rubinstein, in a Western city for a concert, found the grand piano slightly out of whack, but was told that the local tuner, a Mr. Orlando Oppornokity, would have it fixed in jig time. Mr. O. accordingly was summoned, tinkered with the keys, and departed—but Rubinstein was far from satisfied with his handiwork. "Come back, you plumber," he phoned the culprit, "and this time do your job properly." "Nothing doing," was the firm reply. "Oppornokity only tunes once."

15

FAIR GAME
Puns About Sports

A HOTLY CONTESTED
ball game was in progress in a remote section of a Hawaiian
island when a wild boar suddenly bolted from the woods
and charged at the terrified villager playing left field. The
fielder was lucky. At this precise moment the batter rifled
a hit between third base and shortstop. The ball hit the
boar amidships. The boar stopped in his tracks, then
grabbed the ball in his mouth, swallowed it, and vanished
back into the woods.

The umpire proved he was equal to the occasion. He
promptly ruled the hit an inside-the-pork home run.

One of the toughest umpires in the major leagues had
officiated through two tedious, extra-inning games in a
sweltering midsummer Sunday doubleheader, and was in
even a fouler humor than usual when he barged into his
home after 8 P.M. The sight of his curly-headed, rosy-

cheeked little five-year-old son softened the grizzled arbiter's heart, however, and he proposed, "Come over and sit on my lap, my boy, and I'll tell you all about the latest adventures of Batman."

The boy was not intrigued. In fact, he hollered, "Get away from me, you old goat!"

All of which proves anew that the son never sits on a Brutish Umpire.

A Santa Monica sports fan is working on a new kind of all-star baseball team—just what kind you'll be able to figure out for yourself when you hear his first nine nominations: Tenor from the Mets; Holey from the Red Sox; Scalped from the Indians; Chicken from the Braves; Fallen from the Angels; Loot from the Pirates; Feathers from the Orioles; Prayers from the Cardinals; and Doubletalk from the Senators.

At a fashionable golf course, women members were monopolizing the practice tees as well as the regular course, and a couple of angry husbands began deliberately aiming drives and approaches that came as close as possible to the ubiquitous females without actually nicking them. The vendetta got to a point where the greens committee, reluctantly, was forced to post this warning: "Drive carefully. The next wife you shave may be your own!"

At a golf club in New Mexico, a member returned unexpectedly to his suite to find his wife in the arms of the club's major-domo, Señor Juan Engardar. The outraged husband promptly pulled out his gat and shot the intruder, who collapsed at his feet. The club's golf pro heard the shot and rushed into the room. Taking in the situation at a glance, he clapped the husband on the back and enthused, "Hooray for you, Sam! At last you've made a hole in Juan."

The Russian temperament is peculiarly suited to the game of chess. They say that a Moscovite named Droskycharnoff invented the greatest defense in the history of the game. He grew whiskers so long they hid all sixteen of his pieces.

Droskycharnoff got off to a pungent start when he debarked from a transatlantic jet at J.F.K. Airport recently. A fresh reporter clapped him on the back and chortled, "Welcome, Drosky, old boy! Led any good rooks lately?"

A Princeton Junior appeared in the middle of a tennis tourney and asked casually, "Whose game?" A shy young thing looked up approvingly and murmured, "I am."

Britisher Rufus Fligh of Nottingham, reports Clarence Anderson, has fired the starting gun for practically every foot race—pro and amateur—run in England in the past decade.

The editor of the London *Times* gazed admiringly one day at Mr. Fligh in action, his stopwatch dramatically upraised, and exclaimed, "My! How Fligh times!"

A cardshark once had an extraordinary run of big hands

and was smart enough to quit before his luck changed. "Not another hand, gentlemen," he announced firmly as he cashed in his chips. "I intend to fold my tens and silently steal away."

A poker-loving spiritualist wanted another player for a Saturday-night session and summoned the ghost of a departed companion. The ghost was delighted to sit in on the game, and on the very first hand drew five beautiful hearts. He bet his stack.

Unfortunately, one of the flesh-and-blood players had a pat full house and raked in the pot—just one more time when the spirit was willing but the flush was weak.

Old Chief Gnarled Oak, turned millionaire when oil was discovered on his reservation, was powerfully pleased when his two sons were accepted for membership in a swanky Catalina yacht club. For years, it developed, his one consuming ambition had been to see his red sons in the sail set.

16

PUNDEMONIUM
Very Short Puns for People in a Hurry

THE ONLY SON of a billionaire was run over by a steamroller one morning. Of course, the obituary notice referred to him as a compressed heir.

They've designed a new automobile intended only for bucking traffic during rush hours on the nation's throughways. It's called a stationary wagon.

An eccentric bachelor passed away and left a nephew nothing but 392 clocks. The nephew now is busy winding up the estate.

A minister asked a nervous bridegroom, "Wilt thou take this woman as thy lawful wedded wife?" The groom stammered, "I wilt."

Humorist Max Shulman defines croquet as "pure hostility on the lawn," but adds, "I myself play with mallets toward none."

A Texan down on the range is suing for a divorce. He found his dear and an interloper playing.

Tough break for the gymnast who fell off the parallel bars. He was parallelized.

There's a new sandwich shop across the street from the U.N. They call it "The Delegate-essen."

Two cheerleaders ended up at the altar. They met by chants.

Suggested color for all "Keep off the Grass" signs: GWAY.

Two cans of paint got married. Not too long thereafter, the bride whispered ecstatically to her groom, "Darling, I think I'm pigment."

A high school dropout landed a job that takes a lot of guts. He puts strings on electric guitars.

Farmer Klopfer's smartest hen stopped smack in the middle of Route 1. She wanted to lay it on the line.

A publisher who specializes in novels about zombies, goblins, and demons has just established Dybbuk-of-the-Month Club.

Two boy silkworms pursued a luscious girl silkworm. They ended up in a tie.

Home for the holidays from a tough reform school, a teen-age delinquent called out, "Look, Mom, no depravities."

A beauty-conscious maiden has had her nose altered, her face lifted, and wears falsies front and back. Boy friends keep asking her, "What's you, Pussycat?"

There's an eccentric in Asbury Park who spends his entire time throwing rocks at sea gulls. He leaves no tern unstoned.

A kindly doctor assures every patient, "This injection won't hurt a bit." Unfortunately, it's just an M.D. promise.

Charles Rice complains that though he heats his palazzo with oil, his bills are gastronomical.

Nipsy Russell knows a dermatologist who built his practice very deliberately. He started from scratch.

A young exterminator announced that he had invented a new spray, one application of which would remain effective for a full year. "Of course," he qualified, "I've still got a few bugs to iron out."

With construction of a gleaming new skyscraper well

under way, a bricklayer suddenly lost interest in the entire project. So he threw in the trowel.

Advice to ice skaters: You can't always tell a brook by its cover.

They're hoping to launch a new kind of chewing gum for people who simply loathe the brands now on the market. It's called eschewing gum. The same sponsors plan to promote a new cigarette called "Less." Their slogan: "If you can't quit altogether, smoke Less."

"Christmas," sneered a young disbeliever, "is the time of year when bosses throw their dogs a bonus."

"Speaking of bathing in famous springs," said a tramp to a tourist, "I recall bathing in the spring of 1908."

When old seadog Cowles's boat sank, he hied himself to a haberdashery to buy a new yachting cap. The hatter asked sympathetically, "Capsize?" Cowles answered, "Seven and an eighth."

Squire Perkins had an ambitious son who went to New York to make his fortune. The breaks were against him, however, and he ended up as a bootblack in the Kennedy Airport. Squire Perkins continued to work his old farm. Now the father makes hay while the son shines.

Accused of being a lazy good-for-nothing, a paunchy, virtually immobile hillbilly bridled, protesting, "You got me wrong, Mister. I'm a real go-getter. My wife works fourteen hours a day; then I go get 'er."

During a recent downpour, a merchant observed, "It's raining cats and dogs today." "Don't I know it," concurred his partner. "I just stepped into a poodle."

An ingenious postman cut a big hole in the bottom of his pouch, declaring proudly, "The mail must go through."

There's a chap in Coney Island who makes a pretty penny being a habitué. He stands by a scale on the boardwalk, chanting to passers-by, "Habitué 168, habitué 184. . . ."

One of those currently popular Indian gurus hops around a great deal more than his fellow contemplators. That's why he's known as the Kan Guru.

The Old Lady in the Shoe had little trouble keeping her numerous progeny in line. She knew which side her brood should be battered on.

When the great violinist Mischa Elman was born, his ecstatic parents are said to have sent wires to their friends reading simply, "MISCHA ACCOMPLISHED."

A Mr. Bob Campbell of Westwood hired three adjoining rooms at the Beverly Hills Hotel for a business powwow and found a bottle of bitters in one of them. He tried to turn the bottle over to the management, but was rebuffed with "Nay, nay! You must take the bitters with the suite."

A litigant called on the judge for the case one evening during the dinner hour. "I'm sorry," said the maid, barring the door, "but His Honor is at steak."

A hermit in a beaten-up jalopy was apprehended in Pomona, California, whizzing along at eighty miles an hour. The charge, of course, was recluse driving.

An elderly lady hesitated at a busy intersection. A gentleman, noting her confusion, inquired, "Have you vertigo, Madam?" She replied, "Yes, a mile."

In baseball-mad Chicago, Carl Kroch, endeavoring to teach his beautiful wife German, asked, "Was sagst du?" She answered, "They lost, seven to one."

In one year recently the cheese makers of Wisconsin produced two million pounds of Limburger. That's quite a phew!

An old Mississippi showboat captain had eleven children and thirty-two grandchildren. This was one man who bred his cast upon the waters.

Remember the little Dutch boy who saved his country by holding his finger in a hole in the dike until the break could be repaired? They've just discovered what the boy said when grateful citizens pressed him for a speech: "Please, not tonight, folks. I've had a tough day at the orifice!"

There was an unscheduled free-for-all in a Baghdad harem one day when folks in those parts Sinned Bad. The Sultan barged in unexpectedly and his sixty-two wives let out a terrified sheik.

17

WHEN PUNSTERS GET VERSE
Puns in Rhyme

No expert he on freeway speeds
Sober or with cider.
In the graveyard now his headstone reads,
"He crossed the Great Divider."

—C. E. KISER

From Zurich bankrupt Debbie
Sent her pa a little note:
"Every little bit Alps"
Was all the sly minx wrote.

—JOAN WELSH

My Sam said he'd pick me some lilacs
But nary a bloom did he bring.
Though Sam has some points in his favor,
He sure can lilac anything!

—LUCY SHAW

He trod on the corn of the belle at the ball,
And then, so the other girls tell,
Slumbering echoes were raised in the hall
Because of the bawl of the belle.

—FRANCIS DUFFY

You've heard about Indian givers. Well, these two limericks were given to me by two pun-loving Indians:

Just what in the world should we dioux
With that rude and obstreperous Sioux
Who a short time ago
Took an arrow and bow
And raised such a hellabalioux?

"It appears," quoth a miss from K.C.,
"That his Indian blood is the key
To my boy friend's love-making—
And I know he's not faking—
'Cause his grandfather was a Paw-knee."

18

RIDDLE-DE-DEES
Puns in Riddle Form

Q. What did the man say when they told him he'd just become the father of triplets?
A. "I can't believe my census."

Q. In what Texas metropolis is a young lady never quite safe?
A. El Passo.

Q. What do they call call hospitals for parrots?
A. Polly clinics.

Q. What's a crick?
A. The noise made by a Japanese camera.

Q. What's a small dog suffering from chills?
A. A pupsickle.

Q. How do you make an elephant fly?
A. Well, first you take a gre-a-at big zipper . . .

Q. What weighs 2,500 pounds and wears flowers in its
   hair?
A. A hippiepotamus.

Q. Do we get fur from a skunk?
A. Yes, as fur as possible.

Q. What's a good name for an austere hotel?
A. The Waldorf-Austeria.

Q. Who invented the pendulum?
A. Pendulum Franklin.

Q. Who was Alexander Graham Bell Pulaski?
A. The first telephone Pole.

Q. What do they call the Englishman who builds ten boats a month?
A. Sir Launchalot.

Q. What's the best way to drive a baby buggy?
A. Tickle its feet.

Q. What did Paul Revere say when he passed a London barbershop?
A. "The British are combing."

Q. What did the puppy lisp when he sat down in the snow?
A. "My tail is told."

19

AROUND THE WORLD IN EIGHTY PUNS

At one of the early practice blackouts in New York, former Mayor La-Guardia was told that the only thing that prevented a 100-per-cent-perfect result was one little lightning bug who blithely ignored instructions. The Mayor had the offender hauled before him and said, "Why didn't you observe blackout regulations?" "It's this way, Your Honor," said the lightning bug. "When ya gotta glow, ya gotta glow."

Sighed a fair colleen on the eve of New York's annual St. Patrick's Day Parade, "I dreamed I marched up Fifth Avenue in my Erin-go-bragh."

One of America's greatest fiction writers (he turns out market letters for a Wall Street brokerage house) thinks the market goes up along with a rise in ladies' skirts. Glamour stocks and miniskirts soared in 1967; the conglomerates and hemlines went down together in the spring of 1968. This pun-dit's motto: "Don't sell until you see the heights of their thighs."

Near the U.N. there's an apartment house whose tenants include a Mr. Wing and a Mr. Wong. At three o'clock one morning, the latter's phone rang. He picked up the receiver, listened a moment, then said grumpily, "You're winging the Wong number."

The Tappan Zee is the old Dutch name given to a wide expanse of the Hudson River just north of the Manhattan boundary line. In a whimsical mood, columnist Charles McHarry rashly speculated that the name originated via an elderly Dutch dentist in Tarrytown back in the days of George Washington. Said dentist specialized in metal dentures, and to demonstrate how securely they fitted he would invite patients to insert them themselves, then "tap an' zee."

This inspired reader Sam Heffner to assert that in 1789 a plague of roaches descended upon a section of Westchester which won it the name of Roach Hell. Natives promptly shoveled thousands of dead insects into trucks and dumped them willy-nilly into an adjoining community. The cleaned-up town, of course, was now renamed New Roach Hell, and the place where the dumping occurred was yclept Mount Vermin.

A cynical advertising mogul who commutes between New York and Westport on the New Haven the three days a week (maximum) that he works now refers to the beleaguered railroad as "the Anti-Destination League."

There are just two taxicabs generally parked at the railroad station of a town outside Boston, waiting to pick up commuters whose wives are tied up in canasta or bridge games. One taxi is owned by a man named Grady, the other by a man named Slattery, and they detest each other heartily. Things came to something of a climax the other day when, while Slattery was off snatching a beer and hot dog, Grady hung a big sign on his rival's taxi proclaiming, "SLATTERY WILL GET YOU NOWHERE!"

A Bostonian was shown a house by a realtor in Fort Lauderdale. "Here," boasted the realtor, "is the homeowner's dream: a house without a flaw." "Without a flaw?" echoed the Bostonian. "What does one walk on?"

A lovelorn Vermonter stabbed himself with an icicle last winter. He died of cold cuts.

It was at the Atlantic City Beauty Parade. Miss Texas slithered by in her form-fitting white bathing suit. Grosvenor Maitland, Princeton '68, found his heart beating faster and declared, "Joe, this is love at first sight!" "Don't be silly," counseled his friend Joe. "It's just a passing fanny."

A hardy Indian medicine man was dangling his feet from a raft in Palm Beach, watching the great white fathers roughing it in their primitive cabañas. Suddenly a beautiful and voluptuous mermaid popped up from the sea and sat down beside him. The Indian looked her over for a moment and said, "How?"

A little girl in Memphis is a true daughter of the Old South. She's named the live bunny she got for her birthday "Rabbit E. Lee."

"I'm not from Georgia," confided an ardent Senior from Tulane, "but my mother is." "I get it," nodded his hip prom date from Old Miss, "A son of a peach."

On the eve of the year's biggest convention in Detroit, the operators of one of the leading beauty shops went out on strike. The owner managed to keep his temper as long as the girls assigned to picketing his premises were pulchritudinous, but rebelled when he discovered that one babe who was parading back and forth in front of his entrance had been a victim of smallpox. He called union headquarters and roared, "This time you're going too far. My picket has been pocked!"

"You should see what that spendthrift Susan bought at Field's yesterday," reported a Mrs. Goodman in Chicago. "A Ming vase, if you please."
"Maybe," suggested her friend, "she wants it to go with her ming coat."

A butcher in St. Louis got along famously with every

tenant in his building except a mysterious swami who occupied the third-floor rear. How the butcher and the swami loathed each other!

One evening, however, the swami suffered severe pangs of hunger and in desperation staggered downstairs to patronize his enemy's shop. "Give me a pound of liver," he commanded a clerk. The butcher summoned the clerk to the rear of his establishment. "Here's our chance to put one over on that no-good," he exulted. Pointing to his clerk's thumb, he warbled, "Weigh down upon the swami's liver."

A poet in Minneapolis insists that a pond on his farm upstate is the smallest body of water in the U.S.A. He's named it "Lake Inferior."

Omaha devotees of Zen Buddhism went in for contemplating their navels in a big way. A group of them began their contemplating in a studio promptly at three o'clock every afternoon. The leader called out every day at two-fifty-five, "Five minutes to go, gentlemen! Navel observatory time!"

An alert San Antonio restaurateur has this suggestion printed atop the dessert list on his menus: "Remember the alamode."

The boss of the control tower at a large Texas airport, relays H. Overly, warned a pilot that he had a hole in the bottom of his gas tank, and told him to fly upside down to prevent all of his fuel from spilling. "In short," his message concluded, "loop before you leak."

He's probably the same boss who attempted to avoid gallstones by rolling down hills. "A rolling boss," he figured, "gathers no stones."

Workers on the night shift at the Silver Medal granary will not soon forget the time Silas Hood, the slickest handler of grain in all Kansas, lost his footing and tumbled headfirst into a loaded bin in the basement. As he floundered helplessly in the sea of grain, a fellow worker named Clarence Anderson predicted, "Twenty years from now folks will still be talking of the night Hood was in flour!"

A long-bearded prospector marched into an assayer's office in the gold-rush days and planted two whopping nuggets on the counter. The clerk registered amazement. "Well," rasped the prospector angrily, "don't just stand there. Assay something!"

Another old prospector, stranded in the Nevada wasteland, and in a desperate search for water, happened on a dry stream bed, and then came upon another, only to find that one dry, too. "This," he lamented bitterly, "is what I call going from one ex-stream to another."

Three Indian squaws were admitted to a Phoenix maternity ward at the same time. Chief Wampum, head obstetrician, assigned one to a buffalo hide, the second to an elk hide, and the third to a hippopotamus hide (now where did he get hold of *that* one?). At any rate, the squaws on the elk and buffalo hides each produced a six-pound son. But the squaw on the hippopotamus hide mothered healthy six-pound twins. All of which proves, of course, that the sons of the squaw of the hippopotamus equal the sons of the squaws of the other two hides.

There is no more touching tale in all Indian folklore than the saga of good old Chief Shortcake. When he died, the whole tribe mourned and the lamentations of his faithful squaw were heard for miles around. Neighboring chiefs arrived in full pomp and ceremony and announced, "We've come to make funeral for Chief Shortcake." "Not on your life," announced his widow. (Please don't shoot any poisoned arrows at this point.) "Squaw bury Shortcake."

After the Chief had been laid to rest, incidentally, his brother sauntered into an El Paso hock shop, asked the cash value of his tepee, beads, and wampum belt, and explained tersely, "Me Pawnee."

A chief second only in importance to old man Shortcake asked his favorite squaw one day, "What do you yearn for, my treasure, to give you relief from that persistent sniffle?"

Answered the squaw, " 'Tis but a linen cloth for which I hanker, chief."

An artistic Indian erected a new wigwam and decorated

it with costly manufactured baubles, purchased via a mail-order catalogue. His neighbors, miffed because the new wigwam was getting too much attention, disparaged his effort. Sneered they, "Cheap Sioux veneer!"

A lady tourist at an Indian reservation noticed a swarm of kids outside one tepee. "How many children have you?" she asked the obvious father of the brood. "Sixteen," he replied proudly. "My, my," reacted the lady tourist. "Don't you have endless squabbles and arguments?" "Not at all," grunted the Indian. "We just one big Hopi family."

Pat Foley, manager of a bustling hotel on one of Los Angeles's busiest freeways, amuses himself—and hordes of passing motorists—by putting up humorous messages on his electric signboard. One that caused particular comment read, "JUNE IS DAIRY MONTH—TAKE A COW TO LUNCH." The followup was "GUESS WHAT? A COW DID COME TO LUNCH —AND HAD A MOOTINI."

Trouble brewed in San Francisco's Chinatown recently, and one Hop Sung Lee was earmarked for liquidation. The bullet, unfortunately, clipped an innocent bystander, Willie Lee. The following morning Willie's widow received a note: "Please excuse. Mere slip of tong."

In the lobby of a posh hotel in San Francisco, a gaggle of chess players had formed the habit of staging daily contests, with a growing crowd of kibitzers cheering their efforts. The manager of the hotel, noticing that the lot of them were producing not one cent of revenue for the hotel, ordered them cleared out one afternoon. At the height of the resultant hullabaloo, a lady asked, "What's going on here?" That's when a fellow guest, in a punsive mood, contributed this double-barreled classic: "It's nothing, Ma'am—just the manager pulling his chess nuts out of the foyer."

The Volkswagen belonging to a Reed undergraduate in Portland, Oregon, broke down once too often. So he consigned it to the Old Volks Home.

In Seattle, there's a widely read advice-to-the-lovelorn editor, whose motto is "If at first you don't succeed, try a little ardor."

Heading back eastward, we come upon a Duluth fortune-teller who gazed into his crystal ball and told his young lady client that something very amusing was about to happen to her. Then he burst into uproarious laughter. The young lady rose and smacked his face. "Why did you do that?" asked the astounded clairvoyant. "My mother," she said firmly, "always told me to strike a happy medium!"

And back in the fair city of Rochester, New York, Howard Hosmer would have you believe that a young couple received from Australian friends a crated, two-month-old rary as a gift. The rary, not unlike a kangaroo in looks and habits, was cute as all getout, but its appetite was enormous, and as it matured it showed every sign of eating the couple out of house and home.

The Rochester Zoo had all the raries it wanted at the moment, and the young couple reluctantly decided to do away with their Australian beastie altogether. The husband knew a country road that skirted a steep bluff overlooking the Genesee River gorge, and, after borrowing a dump truck for the purpose, dropped the animal over the edge.

Too late, the animal realized his fate. His last reproachful words as he plunged into space were "It's a long way to tip a rary."

A well-remembered friend, West Coast literary arbiter Joseph Henry Jackson, was the inventor of a game that calls for place names particularly suited to the states in which they are located.

Examples, from west to east: Metro, Cal.; Allcomeoutinthe, Wash.; Coco, Colo.; Tyatin, Kan.; Whocouldaskforanything, Mo.; Income, Tex.; Oola, La.; Hittor, Miss.; Praise, Ala.; Fiven, Tenn.; Farmerina, Del.; Hesmakeinizeatme, Pa.; Proan, Conn.; Goodness, Me.

This could go on indefinitely!

Last New Year's Eve, recalls William Travis, world traveler from Birmingham, a neighbor of his named Early gave a costume party, and to insure its success mailed invitations far in advance. Two eager guests, dressed as an old man and a dazzling young girl, to represent May and December, showed up for the party on Halloween. "You've pulled the boner of the year," scoffed the host. "Not at all," corrected the masqueraders. "We're just two months, Early."

In Mexico, an Acapulcan, charged with pushing his wife over a precipice, alibied, "Honest, Judge [or "Juez," I guess], I was barely trying tequila!"

In Peru, a gallant cavalier fished a drowning maiden out of a lake—and married her before the Inca was dry.

In Brazil, an ambitious chap became a member of Rio's overworked Sanitation Department. When he married, he was asked where he had discovered his bride. Softly he hummed, " 'Twas on the pile of debris that I found her."

A top prize for Paralyzing Puns must fall into the lap of the perpetrator of the following horror:

Waitress: Hawaii, Mister? You must be Hungary.

Gent: Yes, Siam. And I can't Rumania long, either. Venice lunch ready?

Waitress: I'll Russia table. What'll you Havre? Aix?

Gent: Whatever's ready. But can't Jamaica cook step on the gas?

Waitress: Odessa laugh! But Alaska.

Gent: Don't do me favors. Just put a Cuba sugar in my Java.

Waitress: Don't you be Sicily, big boy. Sweden it yourself. I'm only here to Serbia.

Gent: Denmark my check and call the Bosphorus. I hope

he'll Kenya. I don't Bolivia know who I am!

Waitress: Canada noise! I don't Caribbean. You sure Ararat!

Gent: Samoa your wisecracks? What's got India? D'you think this arguing Alps business? Be Nice! Matter of fact, I gotta Smolensk for ya!

Waitress: Don't Kiev me that Boulogne! Alamein do! S'pain in the neck. Pay your check and scram. Abyssinia!

FINNISH

Horace Sutton, whose travel books are tops in their field, is a punster of note on the side. Here are the titles of a few of his distinguished pieces: on Cannes and Nice, "Old Man Riviera"; on Tunisia, "Tunis, Anybody?"; on Holland, "The Zee Around Us"; on Hawaii, "This Site of Paradise"; on Japan, "Purely Occidental."

A wealthy gentleman took time out from a world yacht cruise to give his crew a Christmas party in port. He went ashore to round up evergreens, victuals, musicians, gifts, and local notables. When he returned to the dock, he found all the greens installed—but on the wrong ship. "Ahoy!" he shouted. "You're treeing up the wrong barque."

Bridge expert Charles Goren likes to recall the game he once played with Mr. and Mrs. Henry Luce and Miss Lee Wright in the smoking room of the Southampton-bound *Queen Mary*—long before the jet age reduced that once magnificent ship to a tourist attraction permanently moored in Long Beach, California.

Mr. Luce was trying valiantly to make good a bid of five spades, doubled, when the table suddenly collapsed, sending cards flying in every direction. "We never could finish the game," concludes Goren solemnly. "The table went down with all hands aboard."

On his first visit to England, a brassy American tried to crash a party at Buckingham Palace, but was tossed out on his London derrière. Picking himself up gingerly, he observed, "Evidently Britannia will not waive the rules."

J. P. Clifford tells about an extremely conservative Londoner who married a wealthy widow of a bootmaker, and wound up a Member of Parliament. They're urging him to call his autobiography, *The Greatest Tory Ever Soled.*

An American tourist in London, forgetting that traffic

there bore to the left instead of the right, looked the wrong way, and was run down. He regained consciousness in an emergency ward near the Thames and moaned, "Did I come here to die?" "No, sir," a nurse assured him. "You came yesterdie."

A gardener attached to Buckingham Palace stole a chair belonging to Queen Elizabeth and hid it in his greenhouse. He was speedily apprehended and sentenced to reading nothing but puns for ten years, an obvious vindication of the old maxim that people who live in grass houses shouldn't stow thrones.

A shrewd little starlet married an eighty-year-old titled newspaper tycoon who could barely navigate, but owned fourteen sumptuous homes in various corners of the world. She explained demurely, "I love him for his charming manors."

A Broadway columnist, reports *Punch*, visited England and, as is his custom, promptly claimed that all the funny stories in circulation there had been "originated" by himself. "I am always being told one of my own stories," he brayed. *Punch* summed it up as "a plain case of the tale dogging the wag."

In Manchester, a scamp named Sam Rollins became so expert in counterfeiting small coins that he avoided detection for years. Scotland Yard, however, finally caught up with him. On his way to jail, Rollins asked his captor disconsolately, "How did you track me down?" The Scotland Yard man, obviously a night-club devotee of Joe E. Lewis, sang softly, "Sam, You Made de Pence Too Long."

Another counterfeiter's proud boast was "I'm an expert with the bad mintin' racket."

Miss Kitty Enton, who lives away off in Surrey, England —although she may be asked to move after this story appears in print—tells about an old squire who loved to putter about his garden, attended by a Cockney gardener who worshipped the ground on which he puttered.

Two sailors hove into view one day, and the bolder of them hollered, "Hi, Pop, what kind of tree is that you're spraying?"

"It's a peach tree," said the squire.

"You're wrong," countered the two sailors together. "It's a pear tree!"

The Cockney gardener was not used to hearing his master disputed. He shook his finger angrily at the sailors and exclaimed, " 'E knows fruit, salts."

In Aberdeen, a Mr. MacGregor asked the new parlormaid, "Are ye fond of movin' pictures, Jeanie?" "Aye," said she readily. "Guid, lass," he nodded, "then maybe ye'll enjoy helping me get half a dozen doon out o' the attic."

It was in a saloon in Dublin, overlooking the River Liffey, that a broth of a lad, obviously tipsy, objected violently when the barkeep would serve him no more. "I'll have yez know," he shouted, "that I'm the featherweight champion of the Imerald Isle!"

"Be you now?" replied the barkeep grimly. "Well, one more peep out of you, me lad, and out you go—feathers and all!"

At a ludicrously expensive hotel in Paris, an American tourist ordered two boiled eggs for breakfast. The waiter turned up with only one. "I perceive," observed the tourist, "that in la belle France one egg is an œuf!"

There is an eccentric artist in the south of France who cultivates carp in the natural pool in his garden. When the carp attain full growth, he catches them, skins them, and makes gentlemen's wallets out of the skins. He is, in fact, the only man on the face of this earth who is noted for his carp to carp walleting.

In Stockholm, a disillusioned Swede inserted this ad in the local newspapers: "I am no longer responsible for my wife's debts. She has left my bed and smorgasbord."

Stout Norwegian sea captain Peter Swanstrum (he says the crew is always having fun at his expanse) lost a sailor overboard in a storm and saw him swallowed by a whale. The resourceful Captain took after the whale in a rowboat and, by judicious handling of an oar, managed to beat the tar out of him.

Two German lads named Hans and Fritz were proceeding gingerly along a narrow mountain ridge with their mother in tow. Below them was a drop of five thousand feet. Fritz, who was in the lead, suddenly discovered that his mother had disappeared. So he called back to his brother, "Look Hans—no mom."

A hunter in Tsarist Russia persuaded a lady of noble birth to accept his suit. For their wedding supper he shot a wild boar. "My love," he apologized, "I know you are accustomed to caviar, champagne, and roasted peacock, but this is all—" "Enough," she interrupted. "I care not what I eat so long as we are together." Inspired by his bride's gastronomic heroism, the hunter immediately composed the opera that was to immortalize his name: *Boar Is Good Enough*.

A Wisconsin farmer with poor relatives in East Germany heard that a food package he had sent them had never arrived. Putting a brave face on things, he cabled them, "CHEER UP! THE WURST IS YET TO COME."

Now let us consider for a lingering moment the saga of a mighty Soviet commissar named Rudolf Mozoltoff. Rudolf was walking down a Moscow street one day with two friends—a man and his wife—when a drop of moisture settled on his shirt. "It's raining," he announced through his beard. "You're wrong," contradicted the wife. "It's snowing." "No, no," insisted her husband. "Rudolf, the Red, knows rain, dear."

When the Nazis overran Czechoslovakia, a stalwart follower of Jan Masaryk sought the sanctuary of the American Embassy, pleading, "Surely you won't mind caching a small Czech!"

Near the conclusion of World War II, recalls John Pericola, a jeepload of Tito's soldiers was speeding along a sketchy, winding road in the Yugoslavian mountain country. Rounding a curve at high speed, the jeep plowed into an oxcart filled with natives. After the crash, they had the devil's own time separating the jeep from the Croats.

A prominent Turkish-paste man promoted an audience with an old-time Sultan. "I don't think I recall your name," said the Sultan pleasantly, "but your fez is familiar."

One day the learned members of Barcelona's most exclusive historical society decided they should sponsor some kind of fete that would make their fellow citizens more aware of their existence—"something," as their corresponding secretary put it, "that will be grist for our quills." So they settled upon a fete to honor the memory of Don Quixote de la Mancha. Unfortunately, the impresario engaged for the occasion discovered that while he had twelve hundred beautiful maidens available, only six hundred dashing caballeros could be rounded up in all Barcelona. It was the mayor who remedied the situation. Mounting his faithful Arabian steed, he galloped to the home of his great, good friend, the mayor of the neighboring city of Tarragona. "I need your help," he announced bluntly. "How are you fixed for blades?"

The trustees of the Madrid Zoo read that there were only thirty-four whooping cranes left in the United States and determined that they must have one before the breed became extinct. Never mind what Spanish wiles they had to exercise to fulfill their ambition; suffice it to say that a whooping crane was dispatched via air freight in due course, and consigned to the Madrid Zoo.

Alas, when the fool bird arrived at the Madrid Airport, he flatly refused to debark, and the brokenhearted trustees had to return empty-handed to their zoo.

The moral of this story is that cranes in Spain stick mainly to the plane.

An intrepid gob from the Sixth Fleet, on shore leave in Morocco, was dazzled when a veiled beauty, doused with a rare, haunting perfume and bedecked with diamonds and emeralds, fell panting into his arms. A hundred yards behind her charged a six-foot-four savage, brandishing a naked sword and howling like a dervish.

"Queek, queek," whispered the veiled goddess, "which way is the Khan?"

"Lady," said the sailor solemnly, "I'm sorry to say I don't know. I'm a long way from home."

Two scoundrels in Casablanca fleeced the town's richest citizen. As they made off with the boodle, they said, "We must do this Moor often."

A harem-scarem heiress invaded a Tunisian seraglio and demanded a parlor, Bedouin, and bath.

119

An anthropologist in darkest Africa encountered one tribe whose dexterity with spears astounded him. The chief's aim was particularly unerring. When the anthropologist produced a half dollar from his tunic, the chief speared it from a distance of fifty yards. He achieved the same result with a quarter.

"Now," proposed the delighted scientist, "let's see if you can score another bull's-eye on this ten-cent piece." The chief demurred. "These tired old eyes of mine aren't what they used to be," he confessed. "Mind if I let my kid brother try it?"

With that, he cupped his lips and bellowed, "Brother, can you spear a dime?"

An Egyptian guide shepherded his party into Cairo's most beautiful mosque and announced, "Here the sons of our great leader Nasser and his aristocratic friends learn to worship God and his prophet Mohammed." A Maoist from Shanghai interrupted from the edge of the crowd, "That's not the way my Chinese ancestors tell it."

The guide looked pained and remarked, "There seems to be a little Confucian around here."

The scene now shifts to Saudi Arabia, where, according to Ken Suslick of Chicago, an Arab sheik fell off the merry-go-round of a carnival and was promptly gobbled up by the second of three hungry sheep grazing nearby. (Sheep always graze in threes in those parts, it seems.)

The owner of the carnival, angry at losing a cash customer in this distressing fashion, seized the offending animal and exclaimed, "Middle lamb, you've had a dizzy Bey."

Orphaned at an early age, two brothers and their little sister scattered to far corners of the globe. The sister settled in far-off Tibet, where, one day, she smelled something burning. Rushing to the barn, she wailed, "Oh, my bakin' yak!" The older brother became a bell ringer in a New Zealand church. There, one Sunday morning, he got tangled in his rope and tolled himself off.

Another traveler in those parts fell grievously ill and summoned a witch doctor, who examined him carefully, then presented him with a leather thong. "Bite off an inch of this thong every day," he prescribed, "chew it carefully, and at the end of a week you'll be as good as new." When he returned a week later, however, the traveler was sicker than ever. The witch doctor demanded, "How come?" The traveler answered weakly, "The thong is ended, but the malady lingers on."

The maharajah of an interior Indian province decreed that no wild animals could be killed by the populace. Soon the country was overrun by man-eating tigers, lions, panthers, elephants, and boars. The long-suffering people finally could stand it no longer and gave their maharajah an unceremonious heave-ho. As the noted Indian sportsman Mufti Considine points out, it was the first instance on record where the reign was called on account of game.

Back in the fifties, journalistic circles were titillated by the saga of a relative and namesake of Syngman Rhee, then doughty President of South Korea, who came to America to learn the magazine business and enlisted under the banner of Mr. Luce's *Life* magazine. Off on his very first assignment, he succeeded in getting lost completely, and it took New York's best private eyes to track him down.

When they finally spotted him in a Third Avenue café, one cried in relief, "Ah, sweet Mr. Rhee of *Life*, at last I've found you."

A mighty sheik, swimming in oil, was wont to while away a pleasant evening appreciating the gyrations of a native dancing belle named Bubbles. One night, however, a booking agent persuaded him to try Sari, a new importation from Paree. The potentate was so displeased with the substitution that he muttered the sheik equivalent of "Phooey," phoned the agent, and announced curtly, "Sari wrong number."

If it's true, as many pun-dits aver, that the more ludicrous the buildup the more shattering the pun, Don Addis of Hollywood richly deserves high ranking in this staggering compundium for his story of the lad who was counting on his Uncle Al to take him to the circus.

Came the big day, however, and his mother told him that Uncle Al had flown to Australia to see the Davis Cup tennis matches. "I didn't know Uncle Al liked that game so much, Mom," mourned the lad. "Oh, but he does," she assured him. "Many's the time I've heard Alfred laud tennis, son!"

(You will observe that I've discreetly wound up this compundium in Australia. How much farther away from outraged friends in New York can I get?)